COSMOPOLITAN

Sex Confessions

COSMOPOLITAN
Sex Confessions

Real-life steamy sexploits

N A T A L I E   D Y E

ROBSON BOOKS

First published in Great Britain in 2002 by Robson Books, 64 Brewery Road, London N7 9NT

A member of Chrysalis Books plc

British Library Cataloguing in Publication Data
A catalogue record for this title is available from the British Library.

ISBN 1 86105 512 9

Typeset by SX Composing DTP, Rayleigh, Essex
Printed and bound in Great Britain by Creative Print and Design (Wales), Ebbw Vale.

Contents

Introduction

Welcome to *Cosmopolitan*'s collection of our rudest, raciest sex confessions from men and women. Every one of our frank, sin-tillating stories is guaranteed to set your pleasure pulses racing – and is 100 per cent true. From terrific threesomes – and foursomes – to sex in planes, trains and automobiles, our true confessions will sometimes shock and sometimes amaze, but will spice up your bedroom reading every time.

We began printing your amazing sexploits three years ago, when we first asked you to tell us just what you get up to. Since then, our postbag has been bulging with sexy stories. We interview the best, in depth – so you can be sure each story is true and that you won't miss out on a single, dirty detail. It's easy to spot the frauds. Their letters and stories are too well rehearsed, too perfect, and when we question them, there's no real emotion or detail. If it's not true, we don't print it. Each month, we publish the top two stories in *Cosmopolitan* magazine – one male, one female – as 'He Confesses' and 'She Confesses'.

We've found there are two main types of people who confess. First, there are the naughty boys and girls who are up for anything, any time, and are proud to share it. They usually drop us a brief letter, have already told their close friends all the gossip and are happy to chat to us in detail. The second, quieter type are people who've found themselves in an extraordinarily sexy situation and decided – out of character – to go for it. Often, they haven't told anyone until they confess to *Cosmo*. Listening to their stories is like being a therapist, but – they all agree – they feel better for confessing.

Meet the couple who dressed up as Batman and Catwoman, the traffic warden who gave out more than parking tickets, and the girl who discovered her boyfriend's father was bigger and better. One raunchy reader even had a sex romp with an A-list celebrity and his girlfriend. Read on, and find out just what our lustily liberated *Cosmo* readers get up to in – and more often out – of bed . . .

Please note that all names and some details have been changed in order to protect identities.

At *Cosmo*, we promote and practise safe sex. Most of our confessors do too, but we were shocked to discover in our recent *Cosmo* sex survey that 53 per cent of our readers weren't always using condoms on a first date. In response, we've distributed a glossy booklet to universities and sexual-health clinics, underlining our 'passion roulette' safe-sex campaign. Remember: have fun, but protect yourself too. Always use a condom, and keep some in your bag – judging by these naughty confessors, you never know just when you'll need one, or two, or . . .

1
Holiday Heaven

Warm, tanned skin, gorgeous sun-bleached hair and soft, sensual clothes – there's something undeniably sexy about holidays. Add a few cocktails, delicious dinners and stunning sunsets, and who wouldn't feel in the mood for sex? Our *Cosmo* girls – and boys – certainly do.

But it's not always their partner who gets to turn up the heat with our naughty confessors. A lifeguard, a married man on his honeymoon, a stranger on a yacht, even the holiday rep join in their saucy sex-capades when our readers tell all about fun in the sun . . .

She confesses (boy–girl)

I had sex with my pool-side pick-up

Bea was on holiday with her boyfriend but, when a Mr Darcy lookalike beckoned her from his hotel room balcony, she couldn't resist . . .

I saw him in the check-in queue at Gatwick. A pretty Colin Firth. Gorgeous even without the suntan. Very short dark hair, big shoulders, chinos, a baggy shirt – one of those guys who make you feel good just looking at them. No girlfriend, either, just three good-looking mates. Gay? Possibly. He was stunning enough. What really got me was his voice. Deep, posh voices really do it for me. But I was with Neil, so nothing could happen

. . . could it? Three days later we were having sex while Neil was sunbathing by the pool.

Don't get me wrong – I love Neil. We're still together. But after five years, I was going through a 'shall I marry him or leave him?' phase. I couldn't decide whether Neil's obsessive tidiness was endearing or hateful. He'd packed his suitcase a week early, leaving precise gaps for his razor and toothbrush, while I shoved a heap of clothes, strappy sandals and toiletries into mine the night before and had to sit on it to do the zip up. I didn't want to lose Neil, but I did want to do something wild, spontaneous, exciting. Having hot, sticky sex with a gorgeous stranger was perfect. I just didn't think I'd go that far.

'Colin' – I'll call him that, but I never did find out his name – and his friends got off the coach at our hotel. We didn't see them again that day, but in the morning we were all round the hotel pool. Colin looked even better in swimming shorts. They got the beers in and were clearly settled in for the day. Watching him over the top of my trashy novel was really turning me on. When Neil and I had sex that night, I fantasised he was Colin.

It was Day Two when we first made eye contact. I'd glanced over the top of my book, hoping to sneak a peek at him in the pool, and he was looking straight at me. Until then, he'd been a safe fantasy figure, like someone in a movie. You watch them, imagine having sex with them, but that's as far as it goes. Suddenly he was staring back. By the sexy look on his face, he definitely wasn't gay. I don't know who was the most embarrassed. Him, probably, as Neil was sitting next to me – sensibly under an umbrella, of course, as 'you mustn't get too much sun on your second day'. Hmmm. I looked down at my book and Colin dived under the water, but I knew that he fancied me too.

We spent the rest of the day catching each other's eye when Neil wasn't looking. It felt naughty, thrilling. I didn't feel guilty. After all, we weren't actually doing anything – just fantasising about it. That night, I persuaded Neil to stay in the hotel bar, but Colin and his friends only had one drink, then went into town. I told myself to stop behaving like a love-sick teenager. When he appeared by the pool the next day, I planned to totally ignore him. But by lunchtime we were at it again. Then, in an excessively loud voice, he said to his friends, 'I'm going up to the room.'

Neil was dozing on the sunlounger beside me. Colin walked right past me, grinned, and looked up at the balconies above the pool. I couldn't quite believe it. Was he really inviting me up to his room? I didn't think so – my imagination was running away with me. But two minutes later he appeared on one of the first-floor balconies and stared straight down.

The whole idea gave me the ultimate sexual thrill. I was still unsure. For a start, I didn't know him. It could be coincidence, too. But I figured if he was up for it, he'd have his bedroom door open. If I didn't go, I'd never know. So I told Neil I was going to get a drink.

The first-floor corridor was really long, but I could see someone standing by a door halfway down. At first I thought it was the cleaner but as I got closer, I saw it was Colin. I'd thought of loads of sexy lines, but confronted with him, all I managed was 'Hello'. He grinned, led me into the room and kissed me.

The sex wasn't wham, bam – it was actually quite slow and sensual. I knew Neil would never find me in the hotel room, so I took my time. We lay down on the bed, kissing. He undid my bikini top and kissed my breasts for ages before masturbating me. With Neil, I always took the lead, so it felt good to have someone else in charge. He slid off my bikini bottom and gave me slow, gentle oral sex. Then I rolled over and he had sex with me from behind, while I masturbated. We orgasmed together, loudly, and it was only afterwards that I realised the patio doors were open.

We were both pretty embarrassed. I'd taken off my watch, so I had no idea how long I'd been gone. Neither of us said anything about meeting in secret or doing it again. We had a nervous laugh about it being 'one of those things, something we had to get out of our systems'. I was relieved to get dressed and back to the pool. Sex with Colin was great, but when it came to slow, comfortable sex, Neil was better at it.

Neil was sitting up, reading his book. I'd forgotten to buy the drinks but he didn't notice. All he said was, 'You missed a great show. Some couple up there were having really loud sex.' I looked across at Colin's mates. The way they were all suddenly engrossed in their books told me they knew, for sure.

I don't regret having sex with Colin, but I felt pretty uncomfortable about it for the next four days, until we went home. Colin and his friends stayed around the pool, so I developed a sudden interest in going down to the beach every day and eating out at night. It made me realise how much I loved Neil, even if he did have sun creams with factor twenty, ten, eight and four lined up in the bathroom. Ten months on, we're still together.

The last time I saw Colin properly was when we were waiting for the coach back to the airport. We were all outside the hotel. To my horror, Neil got chatting to him. I was so embarrassed that I sat on my own, pretending to look at the plane tickets. Afterwards, Neil told me I wasn't very sociable. Thank God he never found out why . . .

Bea, 24

She confesses (boy–girl)

My sexy holiday rep gave me more than just a welcome pack

Carrie knew sex with customers was strictly off limits for the holiday reps. But she soon persuaded sexy Simon to break all the rules . . .

We'd gone to Greece for a break from men. I'd had it up to here with one-night stands, commitment-phobes and guys who turned out to be, shall we say, an anticlimax. So Sara and I wanted a week of sun, surf and a quiet retsina or two. What I got was sex in our villa, in his apartment, and in the back of his friend's car at the airport.

I spotted him the moment I got off the plane. Sometimes you just can't turn off your automatic radar for good-looking guys. It was baking hot, I had too much luggage, and being herded like sheep onto an ancient-looking coach – clearly with no air conditioning – was not what we'd come on holiday for. But Simon made it all bearable, even helping the driver ram my huge suitcase into the luggage space. The spark was there from the moment he ticked our names off his list. Sara gave me an 'if you go off with him and dump me you're dead' look. I had no intention of it. Holiday reps couldn't have sex with their clients, anyway. It was just fun to flirt.

Simon gave us a talk about the island as the coach careered to our villa complex. He was short and stocky, with sun-bleached hair and a serious tan. I felt pasty and wished to God I'd had an few extra sessions on the sunbed. They dropped us off first, and as we got off, Simon winked and said: 'Don't forget the welcome meeting.' It was that evening, at a bar in the town.

By the time we got there, Sara and I had had far more than

just a couple of retsinas. Our 'villa' was more like a twin-bedded flat. But we behaved ourselves all through the meeting. Afterwards, Simon stopped to chat with each group. This was his third – and last – season as a rep. He was 24, and going back to university to read English. Mmm, educated and good-looking. But he remained totally professional, ignored the fact we'd got quite giggly, and gave out our welcome packs.

The next four days were a typical, relaxing girls' holiday. By the fifth day, I was bored with sunbathing – it's hard to sit still when you work in the city – and itching for something to do. So I went into town and left Sara on the beach.

The tour operator had a small office in the town. I walked past it completely by accident. Simon was inside. He saw me and waved, so I went in for a chat.

I could tell Simon didn't want to fancy me, but he did. He was really serious about his job, but whatever was between us was so intense that you couldn't ignore it. Just being near each other created a real electricity in the air. I knew he would never make the first move, so I invited him to our villa that evening. Sara would go nuts, but I could deal with that. I wanted to take things a step further with Simon and see where we ended up.

I was wrong about Sara. When I got back she was very edgy, and finally confessed that some guy on the beach wanted to take her out for dinner. 'He's got a friend . . .' she added, but I smiled to myself. I'd have the villa, and Simon, to myself.

He arrived in a crisp white shirt and chinos which showed off his sexy tan to perfection. The top buttons of his shirt were undone and I could just catch a glimpse of his smooth, bronzed chest. I had to hold myself back from slipping my hand inside. We had two bottles of horrible Greek wine before I kissed him. It was full on after that. Simon's defences were down, and he really let go. He gently swung my legs onto the sofa, slid his hand underneath my skirt, pulled my knickers aside and masturbated me. After a wonderful, warm orgasm, I unzipped his trousers and gave him slow oral sex. After he came, we lay wrapped in each other's arms for a while, before Simon led me into the bedroom and made love to me again.

Simon was on duty the next morning. He didn't leave until sunrise, so God knows how he got through the day. We hadn't arranged to see each other again, and I couldn't face calling in to the reps' office. Sara wanted to see her guy again. I didn't mind, and having seen his 'friend' on the beach, I definitely didn't fancy a double date. So I stayed in.

Simon turned up, we had one glass of wine and did it all again. This time, being less drunk and more comfortable with each other, the sex was even better. He brought me to orgasm three times – intense, frenzied orgasms. He said he'd never done anything like this before, and I believed him.

We were due to fly home the following afternoon. I wanted to see Simon again, but suggesting it seemed crazy. This was just a 'holiday romance' and I knew better than to try to make more of it. Simon was on the coach taking us back to the airport, ready to greet the in-bound passengers. He told everyone the flight had a three-hour delay.

I don't know how it would have ended without that flight delay. Maybe we'd have said goodbye and that would have been it. But we got chatting in the bar and I whispered something about a 'last fling'. Simon said, 'Come with me.'

We walked out of the airport and across to a mass of parked cars. It wasn't a proper car park, more like a patch of rough ground. He led me up and down the rows until we came to a clapped-out-looking car. Simon pulled out some keys, said, 'This belongs to a friend,' and we got in. It was boiling inside.

The sex was quick, passionate – and hilarious. Trying to get our shorts off in something not much bigger than a Lada just added to it. I ended up straddling him in the front seat, and having the hottest, sweatiest sex of my life.

Simon asked for my address, and I took his. Then we went

back inside, looking pretty dishevelled. Sara knew exactly what we'd been up to, but she didn't say a word. I don't know if anyone else sussed it. I felt sad flying home, and I hoped we would see each other again.

We did, three months later, when Simon came home. He rang me. I'll never know if he'd slept with any other clients, but I'd bet my life he didn't make a habit of it. We went out on a few dates and had some pretty scorching sex in my flat. But it wasn't the same. I wasn't in that carefree, holiday mode, and London in the rain just isn't as sexy as Greece. He went off to university, I met someone at work, and it fizzled out. But I still think of Simon every time I go on holiday – and when I see a rep, I wonder what they're getting up to.

Carrie, 26

He confesses (boy–girl)

I had more than mouth-to-mouth with my female lifeguard

When Mark ran into trouble on his surfboard, his very own Pamela Anderson came to the rescue – in more ways than one . . .

Just don't mention *Baywatch*. I'm a standing joke down the pub. They all know, of course – there are some things in life that you have to share with your mates. Being seduced by a gorgeous female lifeguard is one of them.

It was a scorching day on a beach, somewhere on England's Atlantic coast. OK, it's not quite California, but on a hot, windy summer's day when the surf's up, you'd have to go a long way to beat it. Four of my mates are full-on surfers – they had graduated from their clapped-out student van groaning under the weight of four surfboards to a four-wheel-drive with every boy's toy going. Working in the City does have its advantages.

Call me a wimp – they do – but surfing wasn't my thing. Football, yes; rugby, no problem; but surfing involved driving for hours to the 'right' coast. Sounded like a waste of time. So I didn't even try it. I put up with them talking about it, going off on holidays to do it – and after six years I finally agreed to spend a week surfing with them. I'd just split up with my girlfriend and, to be honest, I wanted the company. Hoped I'd meet a few good-looking girls, too. I never expected wild sex on the beach.

Surfing turned out to be a laugh – and a distraction – even though I was dismal at it. On the fourth day we tried a quieter cove along the coast. We got there early. The tide was out, so it was a long walk across the beach to the water. We passed the lifeguard's hut, slightly up the cliff at the back of the beach. Jon, my mate, stopped to chat about the surf. In the distance I could see another lifeguard wheeling out the flags, showing which areas of the water were safe to use. I couldn't even tell if it was a guy or a girl.

I noticed her the first time I came out of the water. She was sitting on a very tall chair, watching the surfers. The sea was cold, so we were in wetsuits, but she was wearing a red swimsuit with a red lifeguard jacket slung over her shoulders. Blonde hair, tied back, and long, long tanned legs. Looking up at her made them even longer. I wished to God I wasn't so crap at surfing. But the thought of being rescued by her was a total turn-on.

I didn't get into trouble on purpose. Even my mates don't believe me, but it's true. Being inexperienced, I forgot to stay within the flagged area and I drifted across to the right, by the rocks. The current was so strong that you could easily be swept out to sea. The lifeguard bellowed through her loudspeaker. I didn't realise she was talking to me. The next thing I knew, she was beside me in the water, holding a float and yelling, 'For God's sake, get back over there. Have you got a death wish?'

Embarrassed? Me? Totally. I still noticed how gorgeous she was, though. I swam back to the safe area and watched her walk up the beach. My mates were roaring with laughter. How did I feel? Like a right dick-head.

She went back up to the hut and another lifeguard took her place. I thought I'd go and apologise. The door was open and she was drying her hair with a towel. There is nothing more sexy than wet, blonde hair – especially with a tanned, toned body attached to it. She said, 'Oh no, not you again', but she grinned. I apologised. The sexual attraction was instant. I've got to admit, I gave it the big one. Lots of grinning, running my hands through my wet hair – all the tricks that usually work. Come on – I needed all the help I could get. It's not easy to look sexy in a wetsuit. Especially when you can't even surf.

We chatted, never taking our eyes off each other. She offered me a Coke. It was boiling hot in the hut. I took a liberty and asked if I could get changed in it. We both knew where this was heading. I thought she'd back off, but she closed the door, locked it, put her arms around me, pulled my zip down my back and said, 'We'd better get you out of this wetsuit.' It has got to be the hottest, horniest moment of my life.

The hut had windows looking out to sea, with a high table underneath them. The beach was busy, so anyone could see us from the waist up if they turned round and looked. She stood in front, leaning on the table, pretending to write. I pulled my wetsuit down to my knees – it was too embarrassing to hop around trying to get the whole thing off – and put my arms either side of her, leaning over her as if to help. Her swimsuit was almost dry. She reached down between her legs, pulled her swimsuit sideways and began to masturbate. I couldn't believe my luck.

I went inside her straight away. I tried to keep the top of my body as still as possible, so we didn't look too suspicious, but when she began to groan, I couldn't hold back and I came quickly in a few massive thrusts. She was still masturbating, so I stayed inside her until she came. We stayed leaning on the table, then she said: 'Thanks – I needed that. I'll rescue you any time.' I laughed and bent down to try to pull my wetsuit back on, but she handed me a pair of swimming trunks and said, 'You'd better get out of here quick. I'm due back on duty.'

I sunbathed on the beach and then surfed for the rest of the afternoon, grinning at her each time I walked past. My mates didn't believe me. Why should they? She was perched up on the chair or in the hut, totally untouchable, the perfect male fantasy. Then we walked past the lifeguard hut on our way home. Jon cracked a joke about me being talentless. She grinned and said, 'At surfing, maybe, but there are some things he's good at.' Jon was speechless. I winked at her and we left. They were jealous as hell.

Did I go back to that beach? What do you think? Every bloody day. She was there once, but it didn't happen again. I chatted to her in the hut, and we had a laugh about it. She was single and happy – she just fancied sex that day. Right place, right time – and I got the thrill of a lifetime.

Mark, 24

She confesses (boy–girl)

My hot Caribbean dream swam ashore to seduce me

Julie couldn't stop thinking about sex – so when her fantasy man dived off a yacht, she hoped he was heading her way . . .

We'd gone to the Caribbean to 'sort things out'. One of those last-ditch holidays when you know the relationship's doomed but neither of you wants to admit it. After three years, we were like brother and sister. Sex wasn't even comfortable – it was boring. So when a total stranger dived off a yacht and had sex with me on the beach, I didn't feel guilty – I felt exhilarated.

For once, the island looked exactly like the brochure – white beaches, palm trees and gorgeous thatched beach bars. Our single-storey hotel was set back from an idyllic beach, hidden by bushes and trees. The island boasted '365 beaches – one for every day of the year', so not many people used our hotel beach. Also, as I found out the hard way after an early-morning swim, the sea was swarming with jellyfish. The hotel employed a guy to fish them all out, but in typical laid-back Caribbean style, he didn't start work until mid-morning.

The jet lag really got me, and on the fourth day I was still waking up at dawn. Pete was fast asleep, so I walked down to the beach and sat down with my book. We hadn't had sex all holiday. Not even the beautiful Caribbean had rekindled our desire. I was horny, but I didn't want sex with him. To be fair, I don't think he wanted it with me either.

There was no one around, just a small yacht about 150 feet offshore. I couldn't work out if it was moored or sailing past very slowly. A young guy in shorts was standing on the deck, facing the beach. I tried to read my book, but every time I glanced up, he was still there. I didn't feel scared or threatened – I felt excited. I didn't even know if he was alone, or what he looked like, but the whole idea of us watching each other gave me a real thrill. Suddenly, he dived into the water and swam towards the beach.

My first thought was, 'Oh my God, the jellyfish.' I almost jumped up and yelled at him to get back on his boat. But I didn't want to wake everyone up, and also I couldn't be sure he was swimming towards *me*. Maybe he was coming ashore to the hotel. I'd look really stupid if I started yelling. So I played it cool and pretended to read my book, but inside I was buzzing. He got nearer and I knew he was swimming straight to me.

He stood up in the water and walked up the beach, apparently unscathed. I looked up, and I remember thinking, 'This can't be happening.' He was in his mid-twenties and absolutely gorgeous – short, wet dark hair, suntanned firm body, black surfing shorts. I smiled and he said: 'You speak English?' I nodded and he sat down.

It was the most romantic moment of my life. This guy had just swum off a yacht to talk to me. As romantic gestures go, it doesn't get any better than that. Not so far, anyway. He said he was French and spending a few months cruising around on his yacht. I never did find out his name, or what he did for a living.

The sexual attraction was intense from the start. We held eye contact all the time, no matter who was speaking. His English wasn't great, but we didn't chat for long. Suddenly he stroked my neck and slipped my swimsuit strap down over my shoulder. It felt like an electric shock through my whole body. This was what I'd been missing. I prayed Pete wouldn't wake up, put my arms round the stranger and kissed him hard. I bet he couldn't believe his luck – and neither could I.

We fell back on to the sand. Our hands were all over each other. He was still wet, and covered in sand, but the feel of the gritty sand on his body just turned me on even more. He slid down my other strap, kissed my breasts and masturbated me through my swimsuit. I felt his erection pressing against me. I was so horny that I knew we'd have sex there and then, though I couldn't believe what I was doing. I pulled off my swimsuit, pushed down his shorts and masturbated him. He rolled on top of me and we had very fast, very furious and very loud sex on the beach.

Afterwards, we rolled off each other and lay sweating on the sand. He stroked my arm and asked if I'd like to swim out to his boat. But I pointed through the trees and said, 'My boyfriend is in the hotel.' He looked terrified. I've never seen anyone get a pair of shorts on so fast. He kissed me on the cheek, said, 'I love you' and waded out into the water before I could say 'jellyfish'. I pulled on my swimsuit, watched him climb back onto his yacht and slowly sail off, waving as he went.

I was really worried that someone from the hotel had seen us – let alone anyone on the yacht. When I got back to the room, Pete was still fast asleep. No one gave me a funny look at breakfast so I think I got away with it. I never, ever felt guilty. Our relationship was over, and that was one experience I wouldn't have missed for the world. If I ever get down, just thinking about it gives me a boost. My friends were very jealous. Pete and I split up soon after the holiday. Sex on that Caribbean beach was a wake-up call to sort my life out.

Julie, 23

He confesses (boy–girl–girl)

My double-Dutch delight

When his friend dropped out of a double date, David went Dutch with a difference and ended up in bed with both women.

I admit it, this was a 'lads' holiday'. We can be 'caring new men' when we want to be, but Luke and I were single and enjoying it. Spain was the perfect place to ditch the suits, forget about work, chill out with a beer and meet a couple of girls. One for Luke and one for me, of course. I mean, if they both *wanted* to have sex with me, I wouldn't say no. Two girls who were totally up for a no-strings, full-on threesome was my ultimate fantasy. But I didn't think two girls like that existed – until I met Anna and Daniella.

We saw them in a club. Luke was over there like a shot with three glasses of sangria and his best 'hi, girls' grin. Luke's good-looking – girls go mad over him, and he knows it. In the office, I'm the shoulder they cry on, the mug who fields their calls. 'Sorry, Luke's still away from his desk. I'll tell him you called – again.' Luke's not the best relationship material. But as a mate, he's spot on. As a one-night stand, I'd imagine he's even better.

Anna and Daniella were from Holland. Their English was good, and after too many jokes about Holland being full of dykes and big bulbs, we ended up kissing on the beach. I was kissing Anna; Luke was with Daniella. For once, I didn't end up with the ugly one. Sorry to be blunt, but that's the usual score. This time, they were both gorgeous. Waist-length blonde hair, svelte, very big breasts. Anna's were actually the biggest, as I pointed out to Luke the next day. I even got Anna's top off. But the girls weren't going all the way. That was cool. We watched the sunrise, arranged to meet that night and spent the day crashed out by the pool.

Luke disappeared off to the room a few times. Sorry to be even blunter, but we are guys and I figured he'd gone to masturbate. Then he was gone for so long I thought he'd fallen asleep. When he finally emerged, he looked dreadful. Last night's paella had definitely disagreed with him. By 8 p.m. he was still slumped over the loo, saying weakly, 'Go on, mate, you go. I'll see you later.'

I thought Daniella would leave Anna and I to it, but she came along too. Both girls were flirting with me. Sounds crazy, but at first I felt guilty flirting with Daniella. Then I figured she wasn't Luke's girlfriend, so what the hell. I couldn't believe my luck, but I still didn't think we'd have a threesome.

We were all very drunk. I walked the girls back to their hotel. By then we'd all been flirting so much that I didn't know which one I'd end up with. They invited me up to their room. I lay down on the bed and they lay down on either side of me. That's the first time the idea of a threesome became more real. Sure, I'd fantasised about it all evening, but when they lay down on the bed, I knew I was in with a chance.

Anna kissed me first so I rolled over and stroked her breasts, still expecting Daniella to get up and leave. But she didn't. She put her arms around me from behind, kissed the back of my neck and masturbated me. The feeling of Anna's breasts, while being masturbated by Daniella, was the most amazing experience of my life. I almost came. Unless you've done it, it's almost impossible to imagine how incredible it feels.

I turned to Daniella and kissed her, touching her breasts for the first time. If I'm honest, the fact that Luke had been touching her the night before made me even hornier. For once, I was doing something he hadn't. Anna rolled me on to my back and straddled me while I gave Daniella oral sex. Then they swapped places. I don't remember the girls touching each other, which would have been even more of a turn-on, if that's possible. I came inside Daniella as she masturbated to orgasm. I was still giving Anna oral sex, and she came quickly too.

We had sex twice more that night, dozing on the bed in between, and when we woke up the girls weren't embarrassed at all. I've never met two girls who were so comfortable with sex and their own bodies. They knew what they wanted and they got it. So did I, even if I didn't instigate it. I felt guilty about leaving Luke all night, though I know he'd have done exactly the same thing. The girls said maybe we'd 'see each other around'. Luke and I went back to the club, but we didn't see them again.

Sex with Anna and Daniella was incredible. Would I tell a girlfriend about my threesome? I don't think so. They'd never believe I didn't instigate it, or take advantage of two drunk girls, but it wasn't like that. I'd never have had the guts to approach the girls in the first place, so I've got Luke to thank for that. Luckily, they were up for a threesome and made the first move. Luke was gutted. He reckoned they'd have been up for a foursome. I'm not so sure. I didn't fancy seeing Luke with his kit off, either. The way it happened was perfect for me – I was the only guy, getting all the attention. That doesn't happen to me very often.

David, 25

She confesses (boy–girl)

I had sex with a guy on his honeymoon

The man wasn't just married, says Claudia – his wife was waiting by the pool while we were having sex in the hotel bedroom . . .

It was the bleach that did it. Andrew dumped me, you see. Said he needed 'more space'. Crap. He was sleeping with his secretary. Two weeks of tears was long enough. I put 'I Will Survive' on the CD player, turned white-blonde and got some attitude. Even went on the luxury Caribbean break we'd booked, without him. That's where I met 'Scotch'. He was on

his honeymoon. Gave me the come-on. I called his bluff. I
didn't think for a second he'd go through with it. Or that I
would . . .

I still don't know his real name. He was loud, rude and horny.
Scottish, of course. Well over six feet tall, dark hair, huge
shoulders. Serious muscles. Not my usual type, but I was
playing the 'bubbly blonde' to get over Andrew. Loud was
what I needed. He helped me get my huge suitcase off the
baggage carousel. Asked where I was staying. Said 'they' were
staying there too. I turned. She was mousey brown. Shy. Like
me before the bleach. She was quietly telling my best friend
Samantha that they were on honeymoon. That did it. No way
was I getting involved with a married man.

So much for my new 'attitude'. I'd spent the journey in tears,
banging on to Samantha about Andrew. But the white sand,
palms, pool and – if I'm honest – Scotch took my mind off him.
I'd paid for an all-inclusive holiday, so we did the lot. So did
Scotch. His wife didn't. At the disco, he was always up on
stage, leading the games or performing 'YMCA' while his wife
watched silently from the bar, or went to bed. A real mismatch.
I knew he fancied me and I fantasised about sex with him every
night, but I was determined not to flirt.

I blame Ricky Martin. They put on 'La Vida Loca'. Twelve
Martinis convinced me I was the best Latino dancer around.
Scotch couldn't take his eyes off me. His wife had gone to bed.
Watching him watching me, knowing I was making him horny,
really turned me on. I couldn't see his erection but I knew it was
there. I wanted him. Knowing I couldn't – or shouldn't – have
him just made me want him even more.

He sidled up to Samantha and said, 'Your friend really wants
me, doesn't she?' The drink and the blonde hair were a
dangerous cocktail. I wandered over and said, 'You're all talk.
You'd better put your money where your mouth is. Your room
or mine?'

We stared each other out, smiling. I thought he'd cry off, but he replied, 'Better be yours.' There was no way I was going to back down now, so I said, 'OK then, room 440.'He grinned, said, 'See you there at three o'clock tomorrow afternoon,' and walked off.

Samantha and I thought it was hilarious – until we woke up, sober. I told her I'd completely lost the plot. There was no way I could have sex with him. We decided he wouldn't show up anyway. 'You should be there to call his bluff,' Samantha insisted. 'He's such a cocky bastard.'

I saw him at breakfast. He said, 'Hello, girls,' as they passed. So cocky. But if I'm honest, his confidence turned me on. I wanted him to totally take control.

Scotch and his wife spent the morning on the hotel beach. So did we, debating what to do. I'd spent my entire life being shy and anxious about my body. I'd sure as hell never been in a situation like this before. At 2.15 p.m., I made up my mind. The 'new me' was going up to the room to front it out.

Scotch was in the beach restaurant with his wife. He waved at me with three fingers, as if to say, 'See you at three.' But I still didn't think he'd show up. I had a shower, put my sexiest negligée on, sat on the bed and waited. I felt such an idiot.

Just before three, the phone rang. I jumped a mile. It was Samantha. She hissed, 'I'm at the beach bar. He's just left the restaurant, alone!' I was shaking. I wanted him but I didn't think that he – or I – would go through with it.

He knocked. He looked nervous. I said, 'I can't believe you've turned up.' He said, 'Nor can I.' We agreed it was a crazy idea, and chatted for a minute or so. Scotch said he'd better get back to his wife, and leaned forward to kiss me on the cheek. That was it.

We fell backwards onto the bed and kissed. Everywhere. Our hands were all over each other. He was still covered in suntan oil and sand. I rubbed my hands all over his oiled body. It was the loudest, most rampant, frenzied sex I've ever had. I didn't want foreplay – I wanted to feel him inside me. I pulled down his shorts. His erection was enormous. I didn't need or want to masturbate him. He practically ripped my negligée off and climbed on top. I was so wet that his penis slid straight inside me. It felt fantastic. I gasped and shouted out all kinds of dirty words, which turned him on even more. This was pure animal passion, not 'making love' but raw sex.

I knew he was close to orgasm, so I slid my fingers between us and masturbated my clitoris. We came together. It was the loudest, most intense orgasm of my life. Sex had lasted less than ten minutes.

He rolled over, shorts round his ankles, baseball cap and sunglasses still on his head. I said, 'I don't even know your name.' He smiled and told me he hadn't had sex since he arrived. Maybe that was the problem.

He pulled up his shorts and said, 'I'd better go. My wife thinks I'm having a swim. See you in the bar later.' I opened the door for him and peered out, hoping his wife wasn't walking past on her way back to the honeymoon suite.

I had another shower and went back to the beach. He was sitting with his wife as if nothing had happened. Samantha couldn't believe I'd done it. I felt guilty – the guy was on his honeymoon, after all. But we agreed that he was a bastard for doing it, and she was crazy to marry such a Jack the lad. There's nothing like a bit of girl talk to make you feel better.

For the rest of the holiday, Scotch greeted us with, 'Hello, ladies. Been up to anything much?' You couldn't help but admire his nerve. I don't regret having sex with Scotch. It helped me get over Andrew, and gave me the most amazing sexual experience.

As we boarded our flight home, he whispered, 'Fancy joining

the Mile High Club?' The cheek! I told him not to risk calling my bluff again, and avoided his eye on the plane. But I'm sure he would have done it.

Claudia, 24

She confesses (boy–girl)

A Greek sex god rocked my boat

The cruise promised a day of partying. What Anna hadn't expected was no-holds-barred sex . . .

I'm no Shirley Valentine. Put those images of Tom Conti and Pauline Collins making love on a boat out of your head right now. I was 22, and on holiday in Greece with my boyfriend Simon. By the second week, we were tanned, relaxed and almost ready to face the prospect of going home. A day-long cruise with unlimited beer, wine, barbecue and music sounded the perfect way to end it. I didn't realise just how perfect it was going to be . . .

I'll call him Andreas, though I never did find out his real name. We'd seen him around the harbour, chatting up the girls, inviting people onto his boat for a cruise. When the boat sailed back past our hotel each night, around sunset, everyone on board was singing at the top of their voice. It looked a real laugh. A group of English girls from our hotel told us it was the best day they'd ever spent. Now I know why . . .

Simon and Andreas couldn't have been more different, in looks and personality. Blond, blue-eyed, quiet Simon, who – if I'm going to be brutally honest – still had a bit of a problem with coming too soon, if you know what I mean, was the complete opposite of beefy, dark-haired, loud Andreas. Even in bed, as I was to find out. While Simon was all over in three minutes, Andreas was still going after three hours.

Sex with Simon had got better since that drunken first night three years earlier in student digs. A grope in the dark, I masturbated him and . . . whoops! But I really liked him, so we learned about sex together. I taught him how I wanted to be touched – slowly, softly, then faster – and I learned ways to stop him coming so fast. But when he touched me, it was so predictable. Let's just say he wasn't a 'natural'.

The trouble was, Simon had never stopped being a student. Oh, he'd left college alright, and got a job as a dental technician. If I'd heard his tales about 'difficult crowns' once this holiday, I'd heard them a hundred times. But he was pretty immature. Pored over lad mags and wore faded Greenpeace T-shirts. I'd moved on: he hadn't. The holiday was fun, but the distance between us was growing. A year earlier, if he'd gone down with a stomach bug, I'd never have dreamed of going off on the cruise without him. I'd have done a sterling job as Florence Nightingale. But this was my last full day in Greece, and when Simon said feebly from his sickbed, 'Go on, you go. I'll be alright,' I jumped at the chance.

Don't get me wrong here – I wasn't hoping for a mega sex session with Andreas. I fancied him alright, but I was more just up for a laugh. All I had waiting for me at home the next day was a stack of emails, a Monday-morning meeting and a trip to the cattery to pick up Suki, my Siamese.

The boat was smaller than I'd expected, and with fifteen of us on it, we were pretty cramped. I don't know what the rules are about overcrowding, but Andreas didn't seem too bothered, and when another couple turned up on the off chance, he waved them aboard. At first we were all very English about it, trying to give each other space and saying 'sorry' every two minutes, but as the wine flowed we relaxed. Looking back at the white-painted town against the blue sky, I felt I didn't have a care in the world.

I'd heard Andreas speaking fluent English when touting for business, but I guess he figured girls preferred broken English, so that's how he spoke to me on board. Looking back, I admit it sounds corny, but I loved it. Andreas just oozed sex appeal. He was one of those guys you just know will be good at it. A real natural. I couldn't get the thought of Andreas touching me – knowing what to do without being told, seducing me – out of my mind. I realised I hadn't had good sex for a long, long time.

We sailed to a tiny island just off the coast, moored the boat and waded through the shallow water up to the beach. Andreas waved us around to the other side of the island, and when we got there I saw why. The beach was simply stunning – powdery sand, with nothing but sea and sky to look at.

Andreas and his brother fired up the barbecue and cooked burgers while we sunbathed. I'd got to know a few people on the boat, but for once I was able to lie down and relax, on my own, without Simon fidgeting next to me. Heaven. By mid-afternoon, most of the group had fallen asleep on the beach. That's when Andreas came over to me and said, 'You like to come on my boat?'

I thought he meant was I enjoying the trip?, so I nodded enthusiastically. But then he took my hand and led me round the island and out into the water, towards the boat. No one else was around. My head was spinning. I'd had a bit to drink, but I knew what I was doing. Andreas was inviting me onto the boat for sex. 'Come on my boat' meant exactly that. Did I want to? Should I turn back now? No, I wanted it, alright. One look at his tanned, dark body told me that. I didn't know if he was married and I didn't want to know.

We climbed on board. I expected him to lead me downstairs into the cabin, but we sat down on deck and he poured us each a glass of wine. He kissed me, and looked at me sexily with his huge, dark eyes. I'd got so used to sex with Simon that I'd forgotten what real passion can be like. My body was covered in suntan oil and he ran his fingers up and down my spine, making me tingle all over. He undid my bikini top, poured oil on his hands and massaged my breasts, slowly, softly. This wasn't the fast, furious sex I'd expected from him. This was even better. So sensual. I leaned back in the sun and enjoyed every second of it. Bliss. Then I poured oil on my fingertips and massaged his erection. He gripped my hand, so I held his penis harder. That's what he wanted. If I'd done that to Simon, he'd have come straight away.

His body tasted salty, and his shoulders were so big and muscular that I couldn't stop touching them. I pushed my bikini bottoms down, too. The floor was rough and wooden, but Andreas was gentle. He even laid a rug underneath me. We lay down beside each other and masturbated each other just how I liked it – slowly at first, then faster, until I couldn't wait any longer. I pulled him on top of me feverishly and said, 'I want you inside me now.

He'd done it many times before, I could tell. Probably with hundreds of women. But I didn't sense he was comparing me, or judging me – we were just going with the heat of the moment. I don't normally come very easily, but Andreas was a very skilled lover. The sun and the wine relaxed me, and after he came inside me, he masturbated me to orgasm. It was the sweetest, most delicious, most sensual orgasm I'd ever had. The longest, too. When I started to come, he stroked my clitoris so softly that it lasted for ages, with tremors running through my whole body – I'd never felt anything like it.

I'd got a taste for sex and I didn't want to stop. We stayed on the boat making love until the sun began to set and his brother called from the shore to say it was time to leave. We'd have been there all night otherwise.

I'd left my towel and suntan lotion on the beach, so I put on my bikini and ran back. Everyone must have noticed I'd disappeared with Andreas, and there were a few raised eyebrows, but I didn't care. As we rounded the harbour, Andreas started the singing. 'Is good for business,' he grinned. 'People hear you have good time, they want to come too.' I'd come alright. Three times in one afternoon.

As I left the boat, Andreas kissed me on the cheek and said, 'Thank you. You come again on my boat, any time.' Talking about it now, I can hear how corny that sounds. But at the time, on a Greek island, in the sun, it was fabulous. I was going home the next day anyway, but I knew I wouldn't take him up on his offer. The memory of that afternoon was in my mind and I didn't want to do anything to spoil it.

I never regretted having sex with Andreas, nor did I feel used. We both wanted it. Simon never found out, but we split up a month after we got home to England. It was going to happen anyway. I don't blame our difficult sex life – the whole relationship had nowhere else to go. Andreas did more than give me an afternoon in heaven – he made me realise just what was missing from my life.

Anna, 23

2
Down to Business

Talk about mixing business with pleasure. When you're working closely together, under pressure, there's nothing like flirting with your colleagues to relieve the tension. But our *Cosmo* girls and boys take it one step further and find far better ways to de-stress . . .

From giving oral sex at a job interview, to reaching a silent orgasm at their office desk, and getting one up on their arch-rival by giving him the sex of his life in the stationery cupboard, our confessors know just how to deal with that sexy adrenaline buzz. So next time you're in the office, take a closer look around. You never know what people are up to . . .

She confesses (boy–girl)

I had sex at my job interview

When Donna attended an interview for the job of her dreams, she didn't know sex would be one of the tasks she had to complete . . .

It was the answer to my prayers. Five thousand extra a year and a company car. I could pay off my overdraft and go on guilt-free shopping sprees. Restock my make-up bag with Chanel instead of crap. Treat myself to that weekend in New York. All I had to do was make an impression at my interview. Giving my fellow applicant a blow-job certainly did that.

My nerves were buzzing when I arrived at the company's office. It was pretty intimidating – all big leather sofas, deep carpets and real coffee. Fifteen of us applicants were ushered into one room. That's when I saw him. Talk about instant attraction. He was everything I go for, all rolled into one guy. Fair hair, stocky build and an angelic face with a bad-boy grin. Guy Ritchie meets Jamie Oliver. We looked at each other for a second too long – and I knew he wanted me too.

The personnel manager split us into groups of five. Luckily 'Jamie' was in my group. All through the team-building tasks, I had to stop myself staring at him. I couldn't concentrate on my work at all. Every time our eyes met, we grinned at each other. I knew what that grin meant: sex.

The other applicants were trying so hard they didn't notice our silent flirting. I needed this job, so what the hell was I playing at? But I couldn't resist him. The personnel manager set us each five tasks, then left the room. We had 45 minutes to complete them. I glanced across at Jamie and licked my lips. He smiled, and leaned back far enough for his jacket to fall open. I saw his erection bulging in his trousers.

That did it. Job or no job, I had to have him. I was on an absolute high. Jamie said, 'I'm going to take a short break. Does anyone else want some air?' The others shook their heads and carried on working. I followed him out of the room.

The disabled toilet was directly opposite. We went straight in. I couldn't believe I was about to risk everything for a quickie. It was such a turn-on that I felt dizzy with excitement. Jamie kissed me hard and pushed up my skirt. I undid his trousers and masturbated him. His erection was so huge that I knew he was going to come quickly, so I bent down and gave him oral sex, masturbating myself until I was close to orgasm too. He came loudly. I stood up and he quickly brought me to orgasm with his tongue. It was the fastest, most intense orgasm I've ever had. We'd been in there less than five minutes.

Afterwards, we had the giggles. Neither of us could believe we'd done it. He went back to the interview room, but my face was so flushed I had to splash it with water and wait for the red to fade. When I finally walked in, our eyes met and I know we gave the game away. A couple of people said, 'So where have you two been, then?'

I had twenty minutes to catch up on my interview tasks. When the personnel manager came back in, we were split into different groups and I didn't see Jamie for the rest of the day.

That night they called me to offer me a job! I asked who else had been selected and they ran through a few names. Jamie was one of them! I couldn't believe we'd both landed the job. At first I thought I should get his number and talk to him about it. Then I decided to play it cool.

I was dreading seeing him on my first day at work. Luckily, the personnel manager broke the ice. He said, 'I believe you two were in the same interview group.' I replied, 'Yes, we know each other.' Jamie just grinned.

We went to the pub after work and had a laugh about it. There was no way either of us wanted to take it any further, especially as we were working together. We still are. It always comes up when we've had a few drinks, and whenever I pass that disabled loo, I smile to myself. It was the best quickie sex I've ever had.

Donna, 24

He confesses (boy–girl)

She seduced me in a darkroom

Tom's job as a film editor wasn't as glamorous as people thought – until he met Sarah . . .

Tell people you're a film editor and they're usually impressed. Don't get me wrong – it's a great job. But glamorous? No. OK, maybe I make it sound glam when I'm chatting up girls. But most of the time I'm stuck in a cramped, dark, boiling-hot edit suite in Soho for hours on end, cutting the same boring scene over and over while the director has a creative crisis. Not very Hollywood – and definitely not very sexual. Then I worked with Sarah – and found out that spending hours in a small, dark room alone with a gorgeous woman was the biggest sexual thrill of my life. Talk about build-up – by the time we finally had sex, I was ready to explode.

Sarah's reputation preceded her. Not her sexual reputation, of course, but the fact she was a demanding director to work with. I was off on holiday to New York with some mates in three weeks' time, so I'd hoped for an easy run-up. Then the boss said I'd be editing one of Sarah's short films before I went. Oh God.

I admit, I'm normally a bit of a flirt. When you're working in such a confined, dark space, under pressure, a bit of flirting keeps the atmosphere light and makes it more enjoyable. I'd been warned that Sarah had very strong ideas about how she wanted her films to look, and was pretty intense about them, so I figured flirting and light-hearted banter were out. I'd got this mental image of her as a very earnest career woman. Not quite Ann Widdecombe, but . . . No one had mentioned what she looked like, and it just didn't occur to me that she'd be absolutely gorgeous.

The producer showed her into the edit suite and I was completely lost for words. She was in her late twenties, with short blonde hair, huge eyes, beautiful breasts and a pair of DKNY jeans that covered a totally perfect figure. I was too stunned to flirt. Sarah wasn't. She gave me a really flirty grin, and after a couple of days of trying to be totally professional, I flirted back. I'm quite firm with directors – telling them what I reckon will work and what won't – and I think she liked that. She saw me as an equal.

Maybe I was wary of flirting because I was pretty sure something would happen. I'd been with my girlfriend for three years and I didn't want to be unfaithful. Sarah was very up front, the kind of girl who always gets what she wants – and she made it clear she wanted me. Lots of *double entendres* and putting her hand on top of mine when I used the mouse, that kind of thing. After a week in a dark edit suite with her, I wanted Sarah like crazy. I was spending all day in a state of constant arousal, wishing I could just go home and masturbate, and when I had sex with my girlfriend at night, I fantasised that she was Sarah.

Late one afternoon, we got into a heated debate about which of the love scenes in her film should be edited to music. So we ended up watching it over and over again. I closed my eyes so I could hear the rhythm of the music and work out how the sequence should be cut. That's when I felt her hand sliding up my thigh.

I couldn't stop myself. I know that sounds like a pathetic excuse, but I just couldn't. I opened my eyes, and her face was right in front of me. I knew I had to either stop straight away or kiss her. That split second seemed to last for ages. I knew if I stopped, she wouldn't give me the chance again. So I kissed her.

The scene and the music were still playing in the background, so there was a flickering light in the room. She sat astride me and the feel of her pressing down on my erection was incredible. Then she undid my jeans and began masturbating me. I pushed up her top and licked her breasts. That's when I realised where we were. I said something like, 'We can't. Someone will come in.' Sarah whispered, 'We can't stop now.' She climbed off me and wedged a chair under the door handle. Then she gave me oral sex.

I still get off on the memory of being in that darkroom, watching Sarah's head moving up and down on me as she masturbated. By now I was so turned on that I didn't care if the entire staff walked in. Then she pulled off her knickers, pushed up her skirt and we had sex with her straddling me.

I can't tell you how long it lasted because I totally lost track of time. At a guess, I'd say ten minutes. I don't know how I stopped myself coming straight away. When I did come, it was totally explosive and so intense that I didn't even feel guilty. It was one of those sexual experiences you never, ever forget.

We tidied ourselves up and Sarah was putting on her make-up when the producer tried to come in. I quickly pulled the chair away from the door, but I'm sure the producer knew we'd been up to something.

I was amazed when Sarah invited me out for a drink that night – and ashamed to say that we ended up back at her flat, where we did it all again. Sarah confessed that she'd never done anything like it in a work situation before, she just really fancied me. That gave me a kick.

We had sex several more times before finishing the film – though not in the edit suite. Then I went on holiday to New York, Sarah flew out to work in LA and we haven't seen each other since. Looking back, I think there was a massive sexual attraction between us, which boiled over after being in the darkroom for days on end, and we had to get it out of our systems. I'm still with my girlfriend and I do feel guilty about cheating on her with Sarah, but it was sex that I wouldn't have missed for the world.

Tom, 31

She confesses (boy–girl)

I had an orgasm at my office desk

It started as innocent fun, but Mark's sexy emails were so erotic that Jane couldn't control herself . . .

Everyone fancied Mark. He was one of those rare guys with nothing wrong – no wife, no drink problem, not even too much emotional baggage. A great laugh at parties, but caring, too, if anyone in the office was having a hard time. Oh, and I forgot to mention gorgeous.

Sure, I was as sceptical as you are. Mr Perfect, right? Hmm. There must be something wrong. If there was, I couldn't find it. Even his ex-girlfriends still liked him. Maybe he was hopeless in bed. I was wrong again – he got me so horny I had to masturbate at my office desk.

We knew each other well enough to say 'hi'. That was usually by the photocopier. He wasn't the sort to burden his secretary with too much paperwork, and neither was I. See, I told you he was caring. Then he asked me out. It caught me completely by surprise. Did I want to see *Billy Elliot* with him after work? I'd have watched paint dry.

I couldn't concentrate that afternoon, but I didn't tell the girls in the office why. You know what advertising agencies are like – they'd be waiting for me at 9 a.m. wanting a (literally) blow-by-blow account. Luckily I was wearing a black sleeveless dress under my jacket, which looked pretty sexy on its own. I freshened up my make-up, slung the jacket over my arm and met him in a crowded wine bar near the cinema.

I knew when I saw him that we'd have sex that night. The attraction between us was incredible. Sure, I fancied him in the office, but at work he was always so formal. We'd flirted, but it was all very controlled. In the bar, we let ourselves go. The jokes, the innuendoes, the casual touch on the leg – I knew where we were heading. The thought of it made me wet. I just couldn't wait.

We shared a cab home, but we both knew he'd be getting out at my place. I suggested a coffee, and even filled the cafetière. As I pushed down the plunger, he rested his hand on top of mine and kissed the back of my neck. We had slow, sensual sex right there in the kitchen. No oral, no intercourse, but blissful masturbation until we orgasmed together. Mark knew exactly how to touch me – stroking my clitoris slowly and gently, then faster, then slipping his fingers inside me until I was begging him to go back to my clitoris and bring me to orgasm. When I came, it was incredibly intense.

He stayed the night and we masturbated each other twice more. This wasn't a one-night stand, and I wasn't ready for full sex. Sounds crazy, but I wanted to save something for him – and me – to look forward to. I didn't think it would happen the next day.

We arranged a drink for the weekend, and agreed not to tell anyone at work. That suited me. I sat at my computer in a daydream, still turned on by the night before. The sex was so amazing that I couldn't think about anything else. Mark was in and out of meetings, but each time he walked past, he grinned. Then an email flashed up on my screen from 'Mark Brown'. I opened it, expecting a chatty message. But it read, 'I want to come inside you right now.'

He'd taken a risk, no doubt about it. What if that message had scared me off, or turned me off? It didn't. He'd judged my mood perfectly. I was so horny that the words made my clitoris swell. Mark was at his desk up at the far end of the office, behind his computer screen. He leaned around and caught my eye. I licked my lips. Mark smiled and leaned back. I could feel my clitoris between my legs, literally throbbing, wanting him – or me – to touch it. I glanced around, convinced that I had 'sex' written all over my flushed face. But no one was taking any notice. I folded my elbows on the desk, reached inside my jacket and secretly flicked my nipples with my fingers through my shirt.

I had a huge N-shaped desk in the corner of our open-plan office. Sally, my secretary, was the nearest person, about two metres away. The rest of my team sat around a bank of desks on the other side of her. It was 3 p.m. They were all poring over layouts or staring at their computer screens.

I had to masturbate. I decided to go in the ladies' loo. It was too suspicious to go in the disabled one, so I'd have to be quiet. This would be quick – I was already very wet. But I thought I'd better reply to Mark's message first. I sent, 'If you don't stop it I'll come at my desk.' He replied, 'I'm watching.'

My fingers were pretty fast and furious on my nipples now and I squirmed about on my seat, trying to satisfy my clitoris by squeezing it. Mark looked at me. I knew he had an erection. That did it – I was going to masturbate at my desk. I'd never even fantasised about it before, but it was a reality now.

I slid my chair under my desk as far as it would go, with my right arm between my legs. Then I leaned back in the chair, picked up a pencil with my left hand and pretended to make notes. I stretched out my legs and opened them while my right hand slipped inside my trousers. Thank God for elasticated waists. I pushed my middle finger inside my knickers, and when it touched my clitoris, I almost let out a groan. Keeping still wasn't easy – especially the top of my right arm. But knowing that Mark was watching – and that I could be caught – was such a turn-on that I couldn't stop. I kept my eyes on the pages in front of me, glancing up to check no one was coming. I knew I couldn't stay still when I came, so as I neared orgasm, I leaned sideways and pretended to look through my filing cabinet. As I orgasmed, I couldn't stop myself shuddering, so I moved about a bit in my chair to disguise it. They were the most exciting two minutes of my sexual life.

Afterwards, I casually took my right hand out of my trousers, sat up and shuffled some papers on my desk. That was the worst part. I felt sure someone – or everyone – had seen me. My face was already red but now it went even redder. Mark was staring at me with his mouth open. I looked across at Sally and my team, but no one was taking any notice at all. That's when I realised what a risk I'd taken. What if someone had come over to my desk? What if the phone had rung? What did Mark think of me? I couldn't move from my desk for fear they'd all talk about what I'd just done.

Another message flashed up from Mark. This one read: 'You are my dream woman. Let's meet tonight.' That made me feel better – I was up for that. I didn't leave my desk until everyone had gone home. By then I'd calmed down enough to realise I'd got away with it. Mark and I had a good laugh about it – and had fabulous full sex, too. We dated for a few months, and we're still friends. But no orgasm has ever touched the one I had at my desk.

Jane, 30

She confesses (boy–girl)

I had sex with the guest speaker

When Claire attended what she thought would be a dull business function, she didn't know how much fun the speaker would be . . .

I'd seen him on TV. A well-known 'sports personality'. Star guest on sports quiz programmes. Out of ten, I'd say looks got a five, body an eight. Maybe a nine. But he wasn't fantasy material. Just not my type – until the night he was guest speaker at my firm's annual ball . . .

We'd had the dinner, the coffee and far too much wine. His speech was pretty cool – the usual sporting anecdotes. Then he got up to dance. That's when my friend Lisa uttered the immortal words, 'I bet you a gin and tonic that you can't pull the guest speaker.'

I didn't think I stood a chance. His engagement had just been all over the papers. But his fiancée wasn't there, and I couldn't resist the challenge. After all, a G&T was at stake! I didn't plan to have sex with him, just to get him interested.

Our company directors were all over him like a rash. I danced over and gave him the eye. Maybe he was very drunk. Maybe he's the unfaithful type. Maybe he just fancied me. But he was the easiest pick-up I've ever made.

He bought me a drink, and I'd be lying if I said I wasn't flattered. Being chatted up by such a famous guy was a huge turn-on. Ten minutes later, he invited me back to his hotel room 'for a quiet drink'. We both knew what that meant. I was up for it.

There were no press photographers at the ball, but a couple of cameras flashed as we left the party. His hotel room was across our leisure complex sports field. Luckily, no one followed us. Halfway across the field, I asked him his favourite position – genuinely meaning on the pitch. He replied, 'Let me show you,' kissed me hard and thrust his hand up my skirt.

Even though he wasn't that good-looking, the whole scene was an incredible turn-on. I went down on him and gave him oral sex, right in the middle of the pitch, while masturbating myself. I couldn't believe I was doing this with such a famous guy. We were both very close to orgasm and I was going to come, but he pulled me up and said, 'Let's go to my hotel.'

The sex was quick and disappointing. I wished I'd orgasmed on the pitch. We fell on the bed, he went straight inside me and came in a couple of minutes, then fell asleep. By now the alcohol was wearing off, and I didn't even feel like masturbating. I crept out of his room and went back to my flat, wondering why the hell I'd done it. Lisa called the next day and lapped up the whole story.

On Monday morning, when I logged on to my computer at work, there was an email from my boss saying he wanted to see me immediately. He was on the phone, so I hung around outside his office. Suddenly I heard him say, 'I know he's engaged. I don't care if the story is worth £10,000. I've had the *Sun* and the *Mirror* on already. I'm saying the same to you – I've got no comment to make.'

I thought I was going to be sick. How had the papers got hold of it? Had someone seen me giving him oral sex on the pitch? Worse still, had they got photos of it? I didn't know what to do with myself.

My boss called me in and shook his head. He told me to take a seat. Then he spun his chair around and gazed out of the window, over *the* pitch. My throat dried up. Was he going to sack me? Was I going to be branded the company slut? Then he spun round in his chair grinning. Lisa came in, roaring with laughter. They'd set me up. My boss had seen me go off with him, but I don't think he knew for sure if we'd had sex. At least, I hope not.

Lisa took a couple of photos of me dancing with him, and I've got them pinned up on my kitchen wall. We call him the two-minute wonder. I don't regret the experience, but I wouldn't do it again. I haven't seen any stories in the press about him being unfaithful, but I know what he's really like. My boss promised to book *Bullseye* presenter Jim Bowen or someone similar for our next ball, so no worries there!

Claire, 28

She confesses (boy–girl)

I had sex with my arch-rival

Helen hated everything about Peter – until they came face to face in the stationery cupboard . . .

There aren't many gorgeous guys who get my back up, but Peter was one of them. Arrogant, haughty and with a permanent 'I'm better than you' sneer plastered across his face, most of the girls in our company wanted to have sex with him. I wanted to kill him. So the last place I expected to find myself was having sex with Peter in the stationery cupboard.

Peter headed my rival sales team and, with his combination of looks and bravado, beat us hands down most of the time. The words 'no thanks' didn't exist in his vocabulary. I've got to admit, he was the perfect salesman. My sales figures were good, but his were phenomenal. I'd worked damn hard to become a team leader, and the boss thought I was fabulous – until Peter arrived. That's why I hated him so much. Not even his looks could compensate for that.

Our firm's Christmas parties were usually pretty tame: horrible mass-produced roast dinner at a nearby hotel, followed by an appalling disco at which the senior management tried – and failed – to chat up anyone under 30. The sight of my 45-year-old manager attempting a sexy dance to 'Relax' by Frankie Goes To Hollywood wasn't something I ever wished to see again. But being a team leader, I had to go to the party. I thought my team deserved something more, so I suggested an extra party for us sales teams. We could hold it in the office after work, and supply the drinks, crisps and music. What better way to get everyone motivated for the New Year?

By the time the day of our party arrived, I wished to God I hadn't organised it. Our sales teams comprised around 50 people, and I felt totally responsible for ensuring they all had a great time. Rule number one was to keep the wine flowing. Being salespeople, no one had trouble making conversation, and by 9 p.m. we were all – to put it mildly – totally slaughtered. Peter was chatting to three of the girls from my team. They often joked about what sex with Peter would be like, and I knew they all fancied him. Suddenly, I stopped looking at Peter as my arch-rival and imagined how I'd feel if I saw him in a club. I'd fancy him, no doubt about it. Very tall and well-built, with short, almost spiky, black hair, electric eyes and a cheeky grin.

Basically, I saw him as a challenge. After all, practically every woman in the company wanted to sleep with him, and as far as I knew, no one ever had. Underneath his flirty, chatty manner was a guy with smart business sense. He never took the flirting too far and, in the nine months since he joined us, had never dated anyone from work. I wanted to make him want me, but not have me. It started off as a game – a bit of revenge for all those top-class sales figures. I didn't think we'd end up wanting each other so much that we'd have sex an hour later . . .

I disappeared into the loos to touch up my make-up, then strolled over to Peter and the girls and joined in the conversation. Until now, he'd only ever seen me in businesslike mode. I was wearing a low-cut top, so I took off my jacket and gave him the full effect. While the girls giggled, I gave him lots of long, sexy looks – more smouldering than flirting. We ended up talking to each other and the girls drifted off.

I realised I'd spent the last nine months hating someone I hardly knew. Peter was 28, and single since his girlfriend left him a year ago. Maybe it was the drink, or maybe it was because we were talking as equals – not keeping up an image or competing or trying to sell anything, but Peter was incredibly honest. Before that night, I couldn't imagine him admitting to being dumped by anyone. He confessed he'd always found me very unfriendly and standoffish. The more we talked, the more I fancied him, and I was sure he fancied me. It wasn't like a sexual spark between us, it was an intense sexual attraction. I wanted him desperately – and to hell with revenge.

I'd set up the drinks table round the back of the office, by the stationery cupboard. It was a bit out of the way, but until then I'd been doing the rounds with the wine anyway, and knowing how drunk everyone would get, I didn't want the whole lot knocked over. I wanted to get Peter on his own so I could flirt more outrageously without any of my staff watching. So I asked if he'd like to come with me to get the drinks.

The stationery cupboard door was pushed wide open. We both saw it, looked at each other, and giggled. I said, 'Great minds think alike,' pulled him into the cupboard and shut the door. It was almost pitch black, but I didn't bother to find the light. Our hands were all over each other and we kissed hard. I wanted to touch every inch of him.

As we kissed, Peter whispered, 'What if anyone comes in?' I moved round so my back was leaning against the door, holding it closed. Peter pulled down my top, kissed my breasts, then worked his way down, literally ripped open my tights and gave me oral sex. Having to keep quiet made me even more excited, and knowing it was Peter, whom I'd hated so much, gave it an extra edge. I was close to orgasm before his tongue even touched my clitoris, and I came quickly. I turned round, rested my arms against the door and he had sex with me from behind. The door wobbled as he thrusted and, from outside, it must have sounded like knocking, because a split second after Peter came, a woman's voice called, 'Are you OK in there?' Peter pulled his trousers up so fast I thought he'd trap his semi-erect penis in them, and I called, 'Oh, everything's fine, I'm just getting some more wine.'

We both giggled, but I think we both just wanted to get out of there. I certainly did. The sex was fast and fabulous, but the reality of what I'd done hit me. I was worried someone had seen us, worried about facing Peter for the rest of the evening – let alone on Monday morning – and worried that I didn't have a spare pair of tights in my bag. Peter looked on edge too.

I didn't want to put on the light, but I had to check my make-up and clothes were OK, so I snapped it on. My velvet dress was fine but my tights were seriously laddered. I didn't have a spare pair, so I took off what was left of them and hoped no one would notice. I figured the best way was to brazen it out, just in case anyone had seen us, so I slipped out of the cupboard, grabbed two new bottles and launched into the party with, 'Anyone for more wine?' I noticed Peter back in the party a few minutes later.

We didn't speak to each other for the rest of the evening, but we caught each other's eye and grinned. We'd done it! One of the girls on my team, who was very drunk, came up and whispered, 'What were you really doing in that cupboard?' but I didn't let on – though I bet if I had, she'd have been very, very jealous. She didn't even notice the missing tights. I think we got away with it.

To be honest, having sex with Peter did wonders for our working relationship. We were still rivals, but there was a lot more flirty chat – and a lot less nastiness – between us. Who knows, maybe we'll end up back in the stationery cupboard this Christmas . . .

Helen, 30

3
Terrific Threesomes

Who says three's a crowd? Our naughty confessors reveal that threesomes are three times the sexual fun – and foursomes are even better. And if you're going to do it, you may as well do it in style – how about a night in bed with a very famous celebrity *and* his girlfriend? Captured on film, of course . . .

Find out, too, about the chalet girl who admits to giving three guys the skiing holiday of a lifetime after a night 'on the piste', the couples who swapped partners and the girl who gave her boyfriend what he really, really wanted for Valentine's Day . . .

She confesses (girl–boy–boy–boy)

I had a foursome in my ski chalet

Chalet girl Sophie dreamed of having two men in her bed. Three was truly a winter wonderland . . .

Snow, sunshine, skiing, parties, a cool apartment and a different crowd of people every week – that's winter as a chalet girl. You can't beat it. Sure, you've got to shop, cook and clean for the chalet guests, and make a fuss of any sprogs, but it beats temping. Get your schedule sorted and you can still spend plenty of time on the slopes. I'd done it for three years at a well-known resort in the French Alps. The golden rule was 'don't get involved with the clients'. Polite and helpful, yes, but keep your distance. Well, I broke that rule, didn't I? I had sex with three

42

guests. In three years, right? Oh no. In one night, at the same time. If you're going to break the rules, you might as well do it big time.

Our six-bedroom chalet attracted groups, usually couples. My apartment, which I shared with two other chalet girls, was a short walk away. The resort didn't cater much for kids, just serious skiers. I noticed Andy the moment he stepped off the coach. Medium height, and what looked like a hot body under the ski jacket. Mid-twenties, I'd say. What really got me was his hair: almost jet black, dead straight, brushed back off his face. When he reached down to pick up his bag, his hair flopped forward. He ran his hands through it, pushing it back. I know, I know, very Hugh Grant. You've got to admit, it's sexy. Trust me, he was stunning. I looked around for his wife. The Barbie lookalike? No, she was with some forty-plus balding managing director type. Ah, that had to be her – very pretty, with short dark hair. Wrong again. He was clearly with another guy, equally good-looking, but blond. 'Why do I always fancy gay men?' I asked myself, and stepped forward to welcome everyone to their chalet.

Dark-haired Andy and blond Jeff were sharing a room. But they looked embarrassed when they saw the double bed. Both went excessively macho, spoke in deep voices and said, 'I hope you don't snore,' and 'No sneaking over to my side thinking I'm Linda.' So, I was wrong. Turned out Jeff's wife had broken her leg. Andy was a single friend from work. He'd taken Linda's place.

My biggest fantasy was a threesome with two guys. Andy and Jeff fitted the bill perfectly. Of course, I didn't think we'd ever do it, but it fed my fantasy that night. When I masturbated, I imagined Andy and Jeff touching me, giving me oral sex, taking turns to make love to me. My dreams were so sexy, I even reached orgasm in my sleep. It woke me up. Ever done that? I was slightly embarrassed when I made breakfast for the chalet next morning. The dream was so vivid, I felt like we'd actually done it.

I don't want to sound big-headed, but we did get a few single guys in our chalet each season, and a lot of them fancied me. Maybe they thought I'd be an easy lay. About half were 'off the leash', as they put it, leaving non-skiing wives at home. I'd learnt how to deal with them. Say what you like about girl power, but the old-fashioned way was the quickest and best. Enter Francois. Six foot six, pure muscle, tanned, blond, and the best-looking ski instructor in the resort. Simple genetics, isn't it? Survival of the fittest. Show a guy you're paired up with someone bigger and better, and he'll back off. Francois dropped in to the chalet while I was serving breakfast and introduced himself as my fiancé. He wasn't, of course, but that got the client off my back. Andy and Jeff were different. Perhaps I sensed I was going to end up in bed with one of them. I didn't call for Francois. When they flirted with me, I subtly flirted back.

On the last night, the chalet group chose to go out for their farewell dinner. That saved me cooking, and effectively gave me the night off. I could use the food as a welcome dinner for our new guests, so I called in to the chalet after I thought everyone had gone out. Andy and Jeff walked into the kitchen.

I hadn't expected to see them. They'd decided to skip the dinner and go on a bar crawl. Did I want to go with them? Why not? All my friends were working and it was near the end of the season – only two weeks to go. Andy and Jeff would be gone in the morning. What had I got to lose?

We had a great time and got very drunk. Trust me, you'd need to be to do what we did next. Somehow the conversation got on to fantasies. I told them mine. The sexual chemistry between all three of us was totally electric. Until Andy and Jeff, I'd never been in a situation where I fancied two guys equally.

We went back to the chalet, which was in darkness. I wasn't

sure if anyone had come back and gone to bed, so we tried to be quiet. I sneaked up to their room and we drank most of a bottle of Southern Comfort. Then Andy kissed me. We were sitting on the bed when he pulled me towards him and kissed me gently. I kissed him back. Jeff turned out the light and sat in the armchair, unsure whether to leave or join in. I'd never get a chance like this again, so I turned to Jeff and said, 'Come on, Jeff, there's plenty of me to go round.'

I lay back on the bed, with Andy and Jeff on either side of me. Neither of them seemed too sure what to do, so I took the lead. I put Jeff's fingers on my clitoris and his lips around my nipples while I kissed and masturbated Andy. The feeling of two men touching me, taking my clothes off, was simply divine. Jeff worked his way down to my clitoris and gave me oral sex while Andy licked my nipples. I pulled Andy up the bed and gave him oral sex. I knew I was going to come and I tried to stop myself, but I couldn't. The sensation was too intense, too amazing to control.

I didn't stop then. My fantasy was coming true and I wanted sex with both of them. Even after my orgasm, I was still horny. I rolled over and Jeff went inside me from behind while I gave Andy oral sex. None of us heard the door open.

I'm ashamed to admit it, but to this day I still don't know who it was. All the other chalet guests were married or with partners. Had one come back early and we'd woken him up? Was his wife asleep in a nearby room? I'll never know. But I felt him lie down naked on the bed beside me. His body felt young and warm, so I knew it wasn't the older businessman. Mind you, I was so up for it that I wouldn't have cared. Our group sex got pretty wild. I stopped giving Andy oral sex and kissed the stranger. It was too much for Jeff, and he came loudly. I'd never fantasised about a foursome, let alone with a stranger, but this was heaven. I pulled the stranger on top of me and we had fast and furious sex while Andy masturbated next to us. Andy came first, then the stranger. He rolled off me and the four of us lay squashed on the bed, still panting.

The stranger kissed me and left the room. No one knew what to say. I'd had the sexual thrill of a lifetime, but what I really wanted to do now was get my clothes on and get out of there. I waited until I heard snoring, then tiptoed around the room, hunting for my clothes. I never did find my knickers. If either Andy or Jeff was awake, they pretended not to be.

Breakfast was an ordeal. I could handle Andy and Jeff, both of whom avoided eye contact with me and looked seriously embarrassed, but not knowing who the stranger was, and how many other people knew, was humiliating. There was a definite atmosphere, and I was glad when the coach came to take everyone back to the airport.

I said goodbye to each person as they boarded. A couple of the lads winked as they left. They knew. Maybe I'd had sex with one of them. Jeff kissed me on the cheek. I felt guilty because he was married. Andy was last in line. He hung around at the back on purpose, so we had time to talk. He gave me a hug, whispered, 'I still didn't get a chance to make love to you properly,' and gave me a piece of paper with his phone number in London.

I never called. I felt sad about it, because Andy was single and if we hadn't had the foursome, things might have worked out between us. But there was no way I could take it any further, not after what we'd done. At least I lived out my fantasy, and it was wilder and better than I could ever have hoped for.

Sophie, 25

She confesses (boy–girl–girl)

A celebrity filmed me having sex with his girlfriend

Rachel's night of passion with a famous TV star and his girl-friend ended in lights, camera . . . and plenty of action . . .

He was famous, she was beautiful, so why the hell not? Talk about a floor show. We were literally all over his new living-room carpet, masturbating and giving each other oral sex. True to form, he even caught some of it on video camera. He made me swear never to go to the press. No worries there – I don't want my sex life dragged through the tabloids either. I can't tell you his name – though the *Cosmo* girls know who it is! But I can at least tell you about some of the naughty things we got up to that night . . .

I met him at an after-show party. Our company had produced a one-off TV show and he was a star guest. The show went brilliantly and afterwards we all got pretty drunk. Working in TV, I'm used to dealing with celebs, but if I'm honest, I still get a kick out of meeting them. I make a point of chatting to every single one.

He was an outrageous flirt. I wasn't surprised – he had a reputation for it. We only chatted for a few minutes, but his eyes were all over me. I didn't fancy him as much as on TV. What shocked me was when I got chatting to a girl at the bar half an hour later and found out she was his girlfriend. I couldn't imagine flirting like that in front of a partner. But she didn't seem to care. I liked her instantly. She was stunning – short blonde hair, curvaceous, expensive clothes, and generally pretty sussed. If she'd been some long-suffering wife who just sat in the corner and tolerated his behaviour, we'd never have got chatting. But she was outgoing, friendly and flirty, too.

By our fifth drink, we were best friends. I'd never had sex

with a woman, or wanted to – apart from wondering what it would be like – so I didn't look at her sexually. By now I'd missed my last train home and was faced with a very long cab ride, albeit on expenses. But she said, 'Don't worry. You can stay the night with us.'

OK, I admit it. The thought of telling my friends I'd been invited to stay at his house was a real selling point. And I wanted to see inside it. So I said yes. Who needs *Hello!* magazine when you've got the real thing? We had another drink, and she steered the conversation onto sex. Like I say, we were 'best mates' in the way you can only be after three bottles of wine each, so I wasn't totally shocked when she said, 'What do you think about threesomes?'

I knew straight away where this was heading, and I liked it. Couldn't believe my luck. So I was totally honest, told her I'd never done it but the idea turned me on. She said, 'We're into things like this. Are you up for it?' Too bloody right I was. I didn't fancy him that much, but she was gorgeous and if you're going to do it, you might as well do it in style. She looked across at him. He smiled back, as if to say 'OK', and gave me a really sexy look. I realised they'd planned this. That was cool with me. Then she said, 'You realise we'd have to keep it very quiet. The press mustn't get hold of it.' I replied, 'I don't want that either.'

The conversation in the cab was unbelievable. He asked me what sort of sex I liked, whether I was into oral sex, that kind of thing. I told him that I'll try anything once – there isn't much I won't do. The driver had obviously recognised him and was listening intently.

The house wasn't that impressive – he'd recently moved in and it needed a lot of work. We went into the living room, opened a bottle of wine and chatted about his house move. It wasn't awkward small talk – we were all very relaxed, thanks to the alcohol. Then his girlfriend said, 'I'd like to kiss Rachel now,' leaned over and kissed me.

Touching her turned me on, and we slowly undressed each other while he watched from an armchair. She whispered to me that they'd always wanted to do this, but never had. I liked that. I thought he'd masturbate, but he didn't touch himself at all, he just stared. She had an amazing body and I admit I felt a bit self-conscious at first, wishing I was thinner and I'd waxed my bikini line, but as she masturbated me and gave me oral sex, I relaxed and let myself go. That's when I saw him in the doorway with a video camera.

I wasn't happy about being filmed at all, so I told him to turn it off, and he did. I think I was worried that they'd watch the tape afterwards, see my slightly overweight body and think, 'Why didn't we pick someone thin?' OK, I know that doesn't sound very positive and go-getting, but I'm being honest here! She carried on giving me oral sex and I noticed he'd picked up the camera again. This time he whispered, 'Don't worry, it's just for me. I've got far more to lose if this tape gets out.' By now, I was starting to enjoy the idea of being filmed, so we played up to the camera, giving each other oral sex and reaching orgasm right in front of it. That's what he wanted. I was amazed he hadn't even touched himself yet.

Having sex with her was physically great, but there was no emotion – no cuddling or touching, just full-on stimulation. After a while I admit I felt I was just there to fulfil their fantasy. But then, I was getting a kick out of it too, so no one was losing out. The only trouble was that while he was filming us, he kept telling us what to do, like a bloody director. He'd say, 'Suck her nipples,' or 'Give her oral sex now.' His girlfriend tended to do what he asked, but I ignored him.

I lost track of time, but we'd been having sex for ages when he finally put down the camera and lay on the floor beside us. His girlfriend turned to him and took his clothes off. I lay there feeling left out, wondering what to do and thinking we'd all be far more comfy in bed. The new carpet was pretty scratchy. He didn't look all that great with his kit off, and his penis was about average, I'd say, but he'd had so much to drink that he was having trouble keeping it up, so I suggested going through to the bedroom.

We lay on the bed and he asked us to give him oral sex. That was the first time I'd touched him, and I quickly sussed his girlfriend didn't like it. As I licked him, she asked how it felt. I could tell she was jealous, and I didn't want anyone to get hurt, so I backed off and let her take over. He took ages to come, by which time I was getting bored and sleepy. We all fell asleep on the bed.

Next morning I had the hangover from hell, but I honestly didn't feel embarrassed. They were both very laid-back and cool, which helped. We had a coffee, and he offered me a lift to the station in his taxi. I didn't kiss her goodbye, but we gave each other a hug. In the taxi, he was actually very sweet and said, 'I'm worried this will get into the papers, because of who I am.' I promised I'd keep it secret if he never let the tape get out, and I meant it. Mind you, I did let my flatmate in on the secret. All she said was, 'Oh my God!'

I'm glad I did it, but if I had a threesome again, I wouldn't do it with a couple – there's too much risk of someone getting emotionally hurt. If I had sex with a woman again, I'd want it to be more emotional, more caring. But I wouldn't change that night for the world. When I see him on TV or in the papers, I remember how it felt giving him oral sex – and yes, that gives me a real kick!

Rachel, 24

He confesses (boy–girl–boy–girl)

My girlfriend and I set up a foursome on the net

When Jane confessed her ultimate fantasy, Rob went on line to make it happen . . .

It started with Sunday lunch in the pub. Too many drinks later, we were talking unfulfilled fantasies. In the four years that we had been together, Jane and I had tried pretty much everything. But Jane's secret fantasy came as a shock. She wanted sex with another couple. I couldn't believe my luck – my secret fantasy was to watch. So we made it happen – with a couple we met on the Internet.

This wasn't straight wife-swapping. Jane wanted to have sex with the woman while I – and the other guy – watched, masturbating. Sex with your partner afterwards was OK, but no swapping. She couldn't handle seeing me with another woman – and I sure as hell couldn't watch her with another man. But Jane and another woman – definitely! I went hard just listening to it, and when we got home from the pub we had incredible sex on the sofa – raw, hard, fast and far too loud.

The fantasy spiced up our sex life for weeks. Then Jane suggested acting it out. I'd be lying if I said I wasn't nervous. Excited, but nervous. My main fear was getting it on with a couple where the guy was bisexual, or even bi-curious. Sex with another guy turned me right off. And if the guy made a move on Jane, I knew I'd flip. Weirdos and S&M fans were out. But where could we find an educated, good-looking, respectable couple in their late twenties who wanted it too?

Jane was so up for it she asked me almost every day if I'd found someone yet. They had to be strangers, to make sure emotions stayed well out of it. Asking anyone we knew meant word would get out. I didn't even tell my best mate.

I bought a couple of porn 'contact' magazines and we checked the ads. Most couples sounded too old, or into a straight wife-swap or foursome. But one couple were our age, and looking for 'ladies'. I wrote to them with my mobile phone number. The guy called. They lived 60 miles away, but he offered to meet at a hotel in our town.

It was a disaster from the start. I'd put him at forty. The girl was much younger, early twenties at most. I'm sure he was her pimp. She hardly said a word, and obviously didn't want to be there. We had a couple of drinks, said we'd changed our minds, and left. He didn't call again.

The experience did put us off – for a week or two. Then we tried a 'lonely hearts' site on the Internet. Most ads were from singles, but 'Jenny and Alex', from the West Midlands, sounded perfect. 'Professional couple, late twenties, seeks couple for girlie fun.' This time, we were cautious. We emailed each other several times over a month, eventually sending photos and phone numbers. Jane and I described our fantasy and set our boundaries. No wife-swapping and no man-on-man sex. Jenny and Alex were happy with that. They'd done it before. We arranged to meet at a hotel near their home. It was 250 miles away but – we hoped – worth it.

They'd booked a table and arrived first, so the waiter took us over. Jane and I were nervous as hell beforehand, but we felt comfortable with them straight away. Alex worked in IT and Jenny was a PA – similar jobs to ours. We chatted about work, the menu, everything except sex, and got on well – like you do when you meet another couple on holiday. But we all knew this meeting was different.

Jenny was much prettier than she looked on the email, and I knew Jane would be up for it. That excited me. All night, I imagined how they'd look in bed together. When the bill came, Alex said, 'Would you like to come back to our place?' I said, 'It's up to Jane,' hoping she'd say yes. She did. The house was

Victorian, very smart and in a posh suburban street. No one would dream what this couple got up to.

The girls sat on the sofa, and Alex and I took the armchairs. We shared another bottle of wine, then he asked if we'd like to watch 'a film' to put us in the mood. It was soft porn. I watched for a few minutes, then turned round to say something to Jane. She was kissing Jenny.

Jane told me later that Jenny made the first move. They took off each other's tops and I slid my hand inside my trousers to masturbate. I was too shy to masturbate publicly. Alex didn't have that problem – he was already masturbating loud and fast. The girls kissed and licked each other's breasts, then pushed up their dresses and gave each other oral sex. Jane looked over at me several times – I think she was checking I was OK with it. My erection reassured her.

Watching Jane and Jenny was the biggest sexual thrill of my life. I almost reached orgasm so many times, but just about held back. As Jenny masturbated her, Jane began to groan and gasp noisily, and I knew she was going to come. She orgasmed very loudly. I don't know if Jenny had orgasmed or not, but she rolled over towards Alex, bent over the sofa and he had sex with her from behind. I did the same with Jane.

Having sex right next to another couple was an absolute turn-on, like being in your own porn film. I came very quickly. Alex was thrusting inside Jenny while masturbating her. They climaxed together.

Jane and I got dressed quickly, slightly embarrassed, but Jenny and Alex were laid-back and obviously used to it. They chatted to us casually, made some coffee and even offered us the spare room for the night. Jane and I took a taxi back to our hotel, though, and had another mind-blowing sex session.

Sex with another couple definitely improved our sex life. We still talk and fantasise about it. I've since told a couple of mates, who are pretty jealous. I think we were lucky to meet Jenny and

Alex – nice people who were up for it too, and who respected our boundaries. It could easily have gone wrong. We stayed in touch with them by email. Some of the messages were pretty sexual and turned us on. We talked about meeting up again. Jenny and Alex were definitely keen, and if we'd lived nearer, maybe we would have done. But I think we'd fulfilled our fantasy, it was better than we'd ever dreamed of, and there was always the chance Jenny and Alex would want to take things further. We didn't want to risk spoiling it.

Rob, 30

She confesses (boy–girl–boy–girl)

I swapped partners for a night

When Gina accepted an invitation to dinner, she had no idea more than a three-course meal was on the menu . . .

My boyfriend Simon wasn't mad about Rich. I told him he was jealous. Rich had everything Si wanted – the flat, the Audi convertible, the arty job. But, as I pointed out on our way to the dinner party, Rich didn't have me. That made Si laugh. Six hours later, Rich had me on the dining room table – while Si had sex with Rich's girlfriend on the floor.

Joanne always landed the horny guys. They never worked out. They were always more interested in their reflection than a relationship. But she had an incredible sex life. I fantasised about every one of her boyfriends. Then she met Rich. He was the hottest of them all. Si wasn't bad-looking, but Rich was in a different league.

We were drunk. Very drunk. Not much of an excuse, I know,

but we'd had a few bottles of wine at Rich's dinner party. Just the four of us. We'd been dating for a few months, and gone out as a group several times, long enough to feel relaxed in each other's company.

Rich started it. We were slumped at the table, starting on the brandies. Rich said he'd bought a porn film that was so bad it was hilarious. Elevator music, badly dubbed – the works. Did anyone want to see it? Just for a laugh? I wasn't bothered. Si looked eager, so he put it on.

We giggled nervously. Joked about the size of the actresses' enormous breasts. Eventually we fell silent and watched it. I couldn't help getting turned on. Si was shifting uncomfortably, and I knew he had an erection. I looked across, hoping to catch his eye and hint it was time to go, when Rich piped up, 'What's your sexual fantasy then, Si?'

Si blurted out, 'Sex with Joanne.' We roared with laughter. It was usually impossible to get one up on Rich, but he'd done it. Rich got up and walked round to my chair. He said, 'Only if I can have Gina first,' and sat me on his lap. He put his arms round my waist and I felt his erection. I was wet from watching the film but he made me even wetter. Like I said, no one got one up on Rich.

That's when things got crazy. Everyone was trying to make everyone else jealous. Joanne was very drunk but still rattled. She turned off the lights so there was only the glow of the TV, sat on Si's lap and said, 'That's fine with me.'

Si kissed her. I couldn't believe what I was seeing. Every emotion rushed through my head – anger, sadness, despair. Before I could think of anything to say or do, Rich kissed me.

I looked across at Simon. He was fondling Joanne's breasts. Kissing Rich was incredible, but I didn't know what I wanted. My body wanted Rich, my head wanted to get the hell out. I couldn't help thinking I'd got the best deal. Then I saw two women masturbating each other on the TV and my body won.

I slid round on Rich's lap so I was astride him, with my back to Si and Joanne. My clitoris was resting on his penis, and I couldn't stop myself rubbing it up and down. Rich moaned. He took off my top and licked my breasts. I had to know what Si and Joanne were doing, so I glanced round. They were on the floor over the other side of the table. I couldn't see them, but I heard Si grunting and I knew Joanne was masturbating him. It was the weirdest moment of my life. I could either stop now, or go with my body, which was aching to orgasm, and face the consequences.

I pulled Rich to his feet, then I turned round and bent forwards over the table, knocking over a couple of glasses. I didn't care. Rich had sex with me from behind as I masturbated. I could see Si on top of Joanne. I wanted to cry, scream, let all my emotions out, but I was so turned on that the sight of them brought me to orgasm. As I masturbated faster, I was disgusted with myself for doing it. I had no control over my body. When I orgasmed, it was so intense that I let out a cry. Every single nerve in my body was shaking. Rich came immediately, loud enough for everyone to know.

As I came, I was staring straight at Si on top of Joanne. He stopped moving, and as Rich orgasmed, I heard Si say, 'I'm sorry.' He pulled up his trousers, took his jacket off the chair and left, without looking at me. Joanne burst into tears.

I pushed Rich off me, found my top and chased after Si. He was walking down the road in tears. I was upset and angry – after all, he'd started it. Si accepted that. He said, 'I thought I could handle it, but I can't. I'll never forget hearing you and Rich come.'

I haven't spoken to Si since that night, and I still miss him. I don't know what Rich thought about it. Joanne refused to answer my calls and I've heard she still blames me and Si for splitting up her and Rich. I wanted to talk it over with her, because I miss her and I think we were all to blame.

I've still got mixed feelings about that night. I'm disgusted that I did it – and disgusted that I reached orgasm by watching Si and Joanne. It was the most amazing orgasm of my life, and I'm ashamed to admit I fantasise about it, but too many people got hurt. The game got out of hand, and no one stopped it until it was too late.

Gina, 26

He confesses (boy–girl–girl)

She gave me a threesome for Valentine's

Last year's Valentine gift is one Jon will never forget . . .

Have you ever met a guy who *didn't* fantasise about sex with two girls at once? You have? He's lying. Trust me. A threesome is right up there on every guy's sexy wish list. I've fantasised about having one thousands of times. But I couldn't imagine how it would ever happen in real life – until I opened last year's Valentine's card from my girlfriend. She promised me a threesome. For One Night Only.

I'd been dating Ellen for just over a year, since we ended up in bed together after the firm's Christmas party. I'd never seen her before that night – she worked in a completely different section – but her 'look' got me straight away. Long dark hair, slim but with huge breasts and a very sexy smile. Ellen's a girl who knows what she wants and goes straight after it. She chatted *me* up.

I was totally smitten. I'd never met anyone so upfront. Ellen was open about everything, from her breast implants to what she liked in bed. She gave me the confidence to be upfront too.

We'd talked about sexual fantasies, but I didn't confess my threesome fantasy for months. My dream was a night in bed with Ellen and her best friend, Sara.

Telling her was a gamble, I knew that. It meant admitting that I found Sara very attractive, and I thought Ellen might feel I was saying that she alone didn't satisfy me in bed. The night I told her my fantasy, it was just after New Year and we'd had a couple of bottles of wine at home. She was quite giggly and said she'd always wanted to try sex with a woman. I asked who she fancied, expecting her to say someone famous, but she replied, 'Sara.'

Sara was gorgeous, no doubt about it – tall and blonde, small breasts, pert bum. So I wasn't surprised she fancied her. Even though I was drunk, I quickly weighed up my options. I didn't want to upset Ellen, but at the same time, there was a chance that she'd fancy a threesome and make my fantasy come true. It was worth a shot. So I replied, half joking, 'Set it up, then, and I'll join in.'

For a moment, I couldn't tell if it was surprise, shock or horror on her face. Then she put her arm around me and said sexily, 'Are you serious?' There was no going back now, so I kissed her and whispered, 'I've always wanted to try it.' The very idea turned us both on and we had a fabulous sex session on the sofa.

Ellen didn't mention it after that, and I was careful not to flirt with Sara when we saw her in the pub. I figured there was no chance, and went back to fantasising about it.

On Valentine's morning, Ellen left early for work. I gave her a card and flowers, and she told me my present was on the kitchen table – to be opened after she'd gone to work. Inside a huge red envelope was a jokey card, and she'd added: 'Sara and Ellen will be coming round for drinks at 9 p.m. tonight. May your dreams come true.'

It had to be a joke. But I went back to bed to masturbate

anyway. When I called Ellen at work, she said, 'Of course I'm serious. Don't ask any more.'

I had a permanent erection all day. Even frequent trips to the cubicles in the men's toilets didn't relieve it. When I got home I showered, changed the sheets, turned the lights down very low in the bedroom, had several quick drinks to calm my nerves and searched my CDs for something suitable – what kind of music do you play for a threesome? I ended up with smooth jazz.

By 8.30 p.m. the girls hadn't turned up. To be honest, I was angry. If this was a wind-up, it wasn't funny. But the doorbell rang at quarter to nine. I panicked. What would we talk about? Who'd make the first move? I didn't need to worry. They were both giggly, loud and very drunk. Ellen said, 'Come on, Sara, let's do it,' and they took me straight into the bedroom.

Ellen was totally full-on. She pushed me back onto the bed. Sara was giggling and looked unsure what to do, so I took her hand and pulled her down beside me. I wanted to kiss Sara, but I didn't want to blow my chances by coming on too strong, so I whispered to Ellen, 'Kiss Sara.' The two girls kissed across my chest while I masturbated. It was heaven. I'm glad I'd masturbated so many times during the day, or I would have come straight away.

Ellen and Sara kissed and masturbated each other while I watched. I guess at first Sara felt more comfortable with Ellen. Then Ellen gave me oral sex while I kissed Sara. I touched her breasts gently, wondering if she'd push me off, but she didn't, so I moved my hand down and masturbated her. Once everyone had touched everyone else, it was a sexual free-for-all.

During the next couple of hours, I had the most intense, incredible sexual experience of my life. Both girls gave me – and each other – oral sex. I had sex with one while giving the other oral sex, and I came with both of them. If I'm honest, I was more turned on by Sara, as I'd never had sex with her before. The girls brought each other to orgasm twice, masturbating. The sexual kick of watching them was so great that I didn't care that at times I felt slightly left out.

Afterwards, we all fell asleep. When I woke up in the middle of the night, Sara had gone. In the morning, Ellen was very embarrassed, and worried that I'd think she preferred being with girls, as she'd come both times with Sara. I reassured her. I didn't admit that deep down there were times when I had felt left out. But I understood that this was about fulfilling her fantasy – to have sex with Sara – as much as fulfilling mine.

Ellen and I never mentioned it after that day, but when we had sex that night it was very slow and emotional – we both needed something different, something reassuring. When I saw Sara in the pub a few nights later, we were both embarrassed. Luckily, the three of us ended up at a table together. I said, 'So what have you girls been up to, then?' We all burst out laughing. There were times when I wondered if Sara and Ellen ever did it again, which made me feel both jealous and turned on. But I didn't ask. I felt everything that happened that night should stay in the past – though I have told a few, very jealous, mates since.

I split up with Ellen a few months later, when she decided to go travelling. I'll never forget her, especially as she made my dream come true. So when you're writing your Valentine's card this year, promise a sexual fantasy-come-true. Beats an armful of roses any day.

Jon, 28

4
Service with a Smile

From estate agents to delivery guys, personal trainers to window cleaners, vets to driving instructors, our readers come clean on just how personal their service can get. Meet the Catholic priest who dished out tea, sympathy – and full sex. Religion, guilt and repressed sexual desire make a very hot cocktail . . .

Sometimes it's slow and sensual, sometimes it's dirty and rough, but every time brings a whole new, sexy meaning to 'customer service' . . .

She confesses (boy–girl)

I had sex with my patrol pick-up

When Sarah's car broke down, the gorgeous guy in the break-down truck gave her – and the car – a full service . . .

Knights in shining armour really do it for me. The whole rescue, damsel-in-distress set-up is such a turn-on. You'd never think it if you met me. I'm as assertive and career-crazy as they come. But deep down, I've always had this secret fantasy about being rescued. Maybe I watched too many Disney films as a kid. Never confessed it to anyone, of course. So when my car broke down and the most gorgeous, tanned, twenty-something guy was bent over my bonnet, I couldn't stop myself . . .

I admit, greasy overalls and a patrol van aren't quite armour and a trusty steed, but who cares? I didn't. The irony is that I think about sex a lot of the time, but that afternoon it was the very last thing on my mind. I'd been staying with friends for the weekend – one of the huge plus points about being single, you can go where you want, when you want – but halfway back up the motorway, my engine conked out.

Sitting in the car, I was an unhappy mix of fury at breaking down and nervousness at being alone, stranded. Luckily, it was mid-afternoon and still light. I rang my breakdown service on my mobile and even resorted to peering hopelessly under the bonnet. By coincidence, I work as a call handler for a very well-known breakdown organisation – I'll let you guess which one! – but I'd never needed to call a patrol out before. Lads often came to our HQ for training, and the girls and I spent hours sizing them up, awarding marks out of ten. So far, the best we'd seen ranked eight. This time, I didn't care what the hell the patrol looked like so long as they got me out of here, but when he arrived, he was off the scale. Mid-twenties, well-built, tanned, dark hair, dark eyes and a very cheeky smile.

At first he was totally professional, asking what had happened and tinkering under the bonnet. He was very reassuring, and made me feel so safe that my damsel-in-distress fantasy started to kick in and I couldn't stop staring at his bum. Looking at him made me wet. I told him I worked for the company, and that really broke the ice. When I flirted and came out with a few really corny innuendoes – pulling his van up to my bumper was one of them – he flirted back. I didn't want this to end with us swapping phone numbers – I wanted sex. Now. I was sure he did too. In my fantasy, he'd make the first move – but I guessed that in reality he wouldn't risk his job. It was down to me . . .

He got the engine started and said, 'Your fan belt had gone. It's purring like a kitten now.' I gave him my best come-to-bed smile, while frantically thinking how to take it further. Then he said, 'There's a services just down the road. I'll follow you there, to make sure the car's all right.'

It took ten minutes to get there, and every second was making me hornier. Not knowing for sure if he wanted sex – or was just being a very helpful patrolman – added to the thrill. I pulled up in a deserted part of the lorry park, expecting him to wave and drive on, but he parked next to me. He couldn't give me a bigger hint than this. It was now or never.

I got out, knocked on his window and said, 'Go on, then, let's see your equipment.' It sounds so corny, but we'd been laughing at dreadful innuendoes like that. He grinned, and slid across to the other seat so I could get in. I didn't waste time talking – I kissed him.

The sex was very fast and very furious. We kissed hard and he slid his fingers up my skirt, stroking my clitoris and slipping his middle finger inside me, which was heaven. I masturbated him roughly. We were both very loud, and it wasn't quite dark, so anyone driving past could have seen us, but I didn't care. When I was close to orgasm, I bent over and gave him oral sex. I brought him to the very brink of orgasm with my tongue, then he pulled me astride him and we had rough, hot sex right there on the front seat. I masturbated furiously with him inside me, and we came together, very hard and very loud.

We kissed for ages afterwards, with me still on top – I was too embarrassed to get off and face him! The sex was fantastic but I felt like a complete tart. What the hell did he think of me? I said, 'Look, I don't normally do this,' and he replied, 'Don't worry, neither do I. Gives a new meaning to customer service.' We both had to laugh about it. He said he'd got to get back to work, but he gave me his home and mobile numbers and made me promise to call him.

My best friend Sally talked me into calling. Eventually, I sent him a text – and he replied straight away. I was scared he'd given me the numbers just to be polite, but we met up for a drink – even though we live twenty miles apart – and six months on, we're still dating, and still working for the same breakdown service. Sex between us is incredible, though we haven't done it in the van since! It was totally out of character for both of us. People know we met through work, but they've no idea I seduced him by the roadside!

Sarah, 25

He confesses (boy–girl)

We had sex in a show home

When estate agent Phil took Mandy to view a new flat, he had no idea how she'd respond to his hard sell . . .

I've got to admit it: selling houses and flats is a great way to meet women. Single ones, divorcing ones, even married ones flirt with you. I've had women sobbing on my shoulder and giving me the come-on when I value their house after the husband has left. But I draw the line at sex with clients. Getting involved is a big mistake – that's the first rule I teach trainees. Sure, turn on the charm to secure a deal. Flirt a lot, flatter them – you know the score. But that's as far as it goes. Once the contract is signed, you back off, fast. Then I met Mandy – and all my rules went out of the window, along with her underwear . . .

We'd been selling houses and flats – make that 'luxury apartments' – on the new site for months. At first we gave it the full monty – lots of negotiators on site, big ads in the papers, swanky show homes hiding the building site in the background, arty brochures, high-pressure selling. But the site was huge and, despite selling well, we were left with a few apartments that just wouldn't shift at the price. We decamped back to the office and tried selling them individually from there.

Mandy caught my eye the moment she walked in. We've got it sussed at work – if a young guy comes in alone, Sue takes him on. Miss Sexy, we call her. Married couples and women with kids are John's patch. He's Mr Reliable. Young women are split between me and Steve, but when I saw Mandy walk in, I beat him to it. I'd managed, 'Hello, I'm Phil, please take a seat,' before he'd even opened his mouth.

She reminded me of Davina McCall – dark, shoulder-length hair, curvy, big breasts and very bright. Exactly my type. I got a real sexual kick just chatting to her, especially when she took off her jacket and I saw her breasts under her low-cut top. But I kept it businesslike. She flirted first, so I flirted back. Everything about her turned me on, but her sexy smile really got me. Sheer black stockings, too. OK, they could have been tights, but I liked to think of them as stockings – and I found out later I was right. I'd never had an erection while writing down a client's details before.

Mandy was clearly on her lunch break, judging by the smart suit, so I'd have to act fast. She'd just started a new job and didn't know the area. Staying with friends was driving her mad. She wanted a one-bedroom flat, just for her. Thank God – no boyfriend in the picture. I gave her the big sales pitch, while imagining her naked. Did she want to see the 'newly released' apartments after work? The brochure looked good. She was up for it. I told her to come back at 6 p.m. and I'd drive her there. Then I buttoned my jacket before I stood up to shake hands. My erection wouldn't go away and I sure as hell didn't want her – or anyone in the office – to see it.

I couldn't get her out of my mind all afternoon. Most clients, no matter how gorgeous, only enter my head when I'm dealing with them, or a property I think they'll go for. Mandy was different. Steve twigged I fancied her and spent all afternoon taking the mick out of me and being laddish about the whole thing – 'Go on, Phil, give her one in the apartment.' Sure, it crossed my mind. I reckoned I'd fantasise about it later. But I didn't think I really would.

By twenty past six, I figured I'd blown it. Everyone else went home – even Steve, who hung around long enough to tell me I'd been stood up. Then she walked in. Wearing the same clothes, the same perfume, the same come-to-bed smile. I ushered her out the back into my car and we drove to the apartments. Normally when I'm with clients, I'm in 'work mode' in and out of the office. But in my car, with Mandy, it didn't feel like work. I didn't give her the hard sell, I asked how her day had been. We sounded like a bloody married couple, gossiping about work. It surprised me, because I fancied her so much that I thought I'd be nervous, and I wasn't. But I did stare at her legs every time I changed gear.

When we got to the apartment block, Mandy went up the stairs in front of me. Her bum and her legs – in those stockings – were just gorgeous. The flat didn't take long to look round – brand new, spotless, carpeted, no furniture – you either love it or you don't. It smelled of paint and carpets, so I opened the bottom sash window to let some fresh air in. Mandy seemed taken with it, despite the price. She stood looking out of the window. I couldn't blow this. I felt torn. First, there was a good chance she'd buy this flat. We needed to sell it. If I gave her the come-on and she wasn't interested, I could blow the deal – and look like a prat. But if I didn't, I'd never know if she fancied me.

So I dropped something into the conversation. Told her Steve had wound me up all day about finding her attractive. She turned to me and said, 'Do you?'

I didn't know what to say. Come on, I'm an estate agent. The truth isn't always the first thing that springs to mind. I asked, 'What do you think?' She replied, 'If I kiss you, I'll find out.'

The kiss started off slowly. I guess neither of us were sure where this was heading. At first I thought we'd just kiss – I didn't honestly think we'd have sex in there – but things got pretty hot. I felt her suspenders through her skirt and they just drove me wild. She took off her jacket and I felt her breasts. We were still standing right in front of the window, in full view of anyone walking past, and there were no curtains, so I pulled Mandy down onto the floor and pushed her skirt up. Then I pulled off her knickers and tossed them to one side – by accident, straight out of the window.

Mandy giggled and pushed my head down. I knew she wanted oral sex. I masturbated while I licked her, feeling her suspenders with my other hand. Then I turned round and we gave each other oral sex. I came quickly. There was no way I could stop myself. As I orgasmed, Mandy shuddered and she came very hard.

She turned round and lay next to me. I cuddled her, amazed that we'd just done it. When I remember, I can still smell the new carpets and fresh paint in the flat. Then she said, 'I hope you don't think I do that every time I look round a flat,' and I said, 'I hope you don't think I do, either.' We had a laugh about it. She said, 'Shall we knock downstairs and ask for my knickers back?'

I really liked her and I wanted to see her again, but I didn't want to pressure her. By now I didn't care whether or not she bought the bloody flat. So I asked if she fancied dinner at the weekend. She did.

When we got dressed, I looked down at the new carpet. The pile was all neatly vacuumed and flat – but where we'd been it was all churned up. It didn't matter – Mandy bought the flat anyway, and we're still dating after a year. We've even got to know the downstairs neighbours – but we've never asked if they found a pair of knickers on the grass.

Phil, 31

She confesses (boy–girl)

He broke his vows to have sex with me

Celibacy was the name of the game for Father John, but Lucy showed him just what he was missing . . .

We met at a funeral. Surprised? Hardly the most romantic of situations, is it? But where else would someone like me, a finance director, come across a Catholic priest? To be honest, I didn't even notice him until the wake. My aunt and I weren't close at all, especially as she lived in Ireland, but funerals always get to me, and I spent the service in floods of tears. I'm just as bad at weddings. I never leave home without the waterproof mascara. By the time we hit the sherry back at her house, I was starting to feel better. Then Father John walked in – and my God, I couldn't believe anyone so gorgeous would be wearing a dog-collar. Early thirties, short dark hair, huge eyes. Very Mr Darcy – the tall, quiet, brooding type. Why would somebody like that give up sex for life? I'd bet he could have anyone he wanted, with looks like that. Even worse, had he *ever* had sex? My God, if not, what a bloody waste. The thought of him in bed for the first time really turned me on. I know I'm naughty, but I love seducing guys, and you couldn't find a bigger, better challenge than this.

My mother introduced us. Not the best of starts, especially as she speaks to me as if I'm about six, with pigtails and a party frock. Luckily someone called her away, and we were left face to face. I saw it instantly in his eyes. They were huge, clear brown, comforting and understanding. But behind that calm, serene veil, I saw a spark. It was there the moment he looked at me. He held my gaze and didn't look away. Talk about instant sexual attraction. I've had a spark with guys before, but this was bloody dynamite. Maybe he thought he'd perfected the art of hiding his feelings. There was no doubt in my mind that when he looked at me, he thought 'Sex'. I know I did.

We chatted about my aunt. Father John didn't come out with the usual stock answers to life, death and the universe. I found myself doing most of the talking, and being surprisingly honest with him, admitting that I hardly ever saw my aunt but had flown over to Ireland under pressure from my mum. Put up a united family front and all that. He asked how long I was staying. This was my chance to tell him where I'd be. Everyone else was staying in the village, but I'd checked into a hotel in Dublin for three nights. Might as well make the most of it, I'd decided. A bit of shopping, a few pubs and visiting friends who were at uni there. I fished out a box of matches from the hotel, said I'd be on my own and he was welcome to show me around the city. He said he'd be at the vicarage if I needed to talk. Now he *was* avoiding eye contact. I knew, just knew, where this might be heading. When he left, I saw him to the door. We looked at each other for just a moment too long. No one else would have noticed it. There was a sexual hunger, a need, and I'd bet my life he went home to masturbate. I did.

He didn't call. Not surprising, really. Out of sight was out of mind, and he had taken a vow of celibacy, for God's sake. But I couldn't get him out of my head. OK, I admit, the idea of seducing him had started as a challenge. But now I felt compelled to be near him. I needed him, wanted him, and I couldn't control it. So I went round to the vicarage at lunchtime. I thought he'd be taking a service or out visiting, but he answered the door. I'd got a 'I'm lonely, I wondered if we could chat' story all ready, but when we looked at each other, I couldn't bring myself to lie. I sensed we both knew why I was there. He simply said, 'Why don't you come in?' and I sat down on the sofa.

He brought in two mugs of tea and I noticed he wasn't wearing his dog-collar. Turned out Friday was his day off. I apologised for disturbing him, and then I said, 'Why don't you show me around town, if you're free?' He looked relieved when I said that, dumped the tea, grabbed his coat and we got into my hire car. That convinced me. Being alone with me was making him uneasy. He wasn't sure he could control himself either.

We walked around town and ended up on a park bench, facing each other as we talked. Talked is the right word – this wasn't chat. We didn't really flirt, it was far too intense for that. By now it was dark, but the park was well lit and I felt safe with him. He asked about my job, my life in London. I asked why he'd become a priest. Jilted by a girl at sixteen. Broke his heart. In Ireland, the priesthood seemed a good option. Did he regret it? Lately, he'd been thinking deeply about his 'calling'. I sensed my arrival was adding to that. Did he miss intimacy? I didn't give him a chance to answer – I put my arms around his neck and kissed him.

If he was struggling about what to do, I didn't sense it. He kissed me back hard, and from that moment he was full-on. We kissed each other all over our mouths and faces. I wanted to suggest going back to my hotel, but I didn't want to stop and give him a chance to realise what we were doing, so I slid my hand down to feel him. His penis was rock hard, and as I rubbed it, he came almost instantly inside his trousers. I'd heard of premature ejaculation but this was within seconds!

OK, I was disappointed, though I didn't show it. All I could think was, 'He's got what he wants, now he'll apologise and go home.' I was wrong. Not about apologising, which he did profusely, with pointless and unnecessary explanation – I mean, I did *know* he was a celibate priest – but about going home. I whispered softly, 'Why don't you come back to my hotel?' He nodded, so we went. It felt so simple, so right – for me, anyway.

I figured we could raid the mini-bar, relax and maybe, just maybe, carry on where we left off. But we didn't even make it to the mini-bar. As we came through the door, his arms were round me. I was still horny from earlier, so we fell down onto the floor. I never did find out if he'd ever had sex, but he certainly knew what to do. He masturbated me, then climbed on top and we had sex until I was practically raw from the rough carpet. I turned over and he took me from behind, while I masturbated. We came together. I remember him shouting, 'Oh my God' as he came, which almost made me laugh, as I thought it was totally inappropriate under the circumstances.

Afterwards I felt completely sexually satisfied, but nervous about what would happen next. We shared a Coke from the mini-bar and I turned on the TV, but we were both edgy. To be honest, I just wanted him to leave. I felt guilty that I'd seduced him, but then again, we were both adults and he was just as much to blame as me. I also sensed that there was a lot going on in his mind about what he wanted to do, and I didn't want to get involved in those kind of decisions.

Eventually he said, 'Do you mind if I leave? I've got a lot of thinking to do.' I was very relieved. He said something about taking my number in London, but I said, 'Look, we both know this was just sex. Let's leave it at that.' He looked relieved.

I took an earlier flight home the next day, and I never did find out what happened to him. My relatives haven't mentioned any scandal, so for all I know he's still the village priest. I'm bound to go back there sometime for a family wedding or funeral, so I'll probably see him again. It was pure lust, pure animal attraction, between us, nothing more. Who knows whether we'll be able to control ourselves next time?

Lucy, 29

She confesses (boy–girl)

My sex-tastic session with the delivery man

When he arrived with her washing machine, Linda didn't expect a free service . . .

He was Robbie Williams meets Craig from *Big Brother*. Dark hair, tanned body, muscles that wanted to rip their way out of his vest. Sweaty, too, after lugging my new washing machine up four floors. Half an hour later, he was having sex with me from behind as I bent over it.

I wanted him the moment he turned up at my flat, waving his delivery notice with a casual, 'Sign here, love.' Mmm. He wasn't getting away that easily.

Five minutes earlier, I'd been in the mood from hell. The delivery firm gave me a pathetic time slot – 'we'll be there between noon and 6 p.m., darlin'' – which meant taking a day off work and hanging around the flat, bored. It was times like that when I hated my ex, David. He'd moved out six months earlier wanting 'personal space'. Last seen heading for India to 'find himself' – leaving me with the bills, the hassle and the knackered washing machine.

By mid-afternoon, I'd finished my book, played that CD I bought weeks ago, watered my plants (a first – how do they survive?), painted my nails, played with my vibrator (twice) and called everyone in my phone book. I even rang the office 'to see how it's going'.

By 6.30 p.m., I was at boiling point. They weren't coming, I knew it. I'd wasted a whole bloody day. The company was on answerphone. It was a balmy summer evening, perfect for a drink by the river, not stuck in my flat, muttering to myself. So I called a girlfriend and arranged to meet at 8 p.m. Just time for a quick shower. As I stepped out of it, the intercom buzzed.

'Hello, love, we've got your washing machine.' How dare he sound so bloody chirpy? I grunted and buzzed the door. My flat was on the top floor, up four, very twisty flights of stairs. Serves him right.

I pulled on a short shift dress, my strappy sandals and towel-dried my hair. By the time they'd struggled up to my landing, I'd blow-dried it, finished my make-up and was ready to go out. Then I opened the door and saw him.

Put together the best bits of Robbie and Craig and you've got him. A body to die for, glistening with sweat and a real suntan – the kind you get from being outdoors. Not like David's carroty sunbed glow. I hadn't had sex for six months, and suddenly I knew it. His eyes told me he wanted it too. This was total lust, pure animal attraction. For a split second I stood still, not knowing what to do. Then I blurted out, 'I'm Linda.'

He grinned and looked me up and down. Normally I'd hate a guy doing that, but this time I did it back. I'd never been so upfront with anyone in my life. He was impressed. I licked my lips and was about to ask him in 'for a Coke' when a big fat hulk of a guy appeared at the top of the stairs with a trolley and said, 'God, Joe, that was a heavy bastard. Where d'you want it, love?'

My fantasy was in ruins. There was no way we'd have sex now. Not with Meatloaf in tow. I was so up for it that if the second guy had resembled Robbie, Craig or even Jamie Oliver, I'd have tried out my threesome fantasy. But he didn't. If Joe was a built-in automatic, he was a twin tub. I pointed to the kitchen and Meatloaf wheeled my machine through while Joe said, 'Sign here, love.'

His accent was pure cockney, very rough-and-ready. I was getting hornier by the second. I didn't want a relationship, or even his number. What I wanted was sex, with him, right now. I handed back the signed form with one hand, and ran the middle finger of my other hand up the inside of his thigh. This was a first for me. But I'd spent too long worrying about what David wanted, what everyone else wanted. This was about me. I wanted Joe, and I'd make him want me.

I ran my finger slowly across his balls and up his flies. His erection got harder by the second. When I felt the top of his penis, I stroked from side to side. He groaned. I said, 'Can you get rid of your mate?' Joe disappeared into the kitchen. I can guess what he said, but I didn't care. Meatloaf said, 'I'll, er, take the trolley back to the van,' and winked at me. I smiled and shut the door behind him.

We didn't waste time. Joe was sitting on top of the washing machine in the middle of the kitchen. He asked if I was expecting anyone home. I shook my head and ran my hands up his thighs. He pulled me towards him and kissed me hard. He tasted of coffee and cigarettes, so different to David. But that's what I wanted. His hands were all over me, pushing up my dress and into my knickers. When his fingers roughly rubbed my clitoris, I thought I was going to orgasm.

I pulled him off the washing machine, unzipped his trousers and gave him oral sex. Joe grunted and moaned so loudly that I prayed the neighbours were out. When he was close to orgasm, he pulled me to my feet, turned me round, bent me over the washing machine and entered me from behind. His penis was long and wide, and it felt so good inside me. His thrusts were fast and furious, and I knew he'd come quickly, so I masturbated myself to orgasm too. By now I was moaning even more loudly than him. When he came, his whole body shook, and I came too, harder than I ever had before.

I half-expected him to pull up his trousers and leave, but he was really sweet. He said, 'You go and have a shower. I'll plumb in the washing machine. Better check it still works.'

In the shower, I was pretty amazed I'd done it. Then I felt really embarrassed and figured I'd stay in there until he left. But I'd left cash and credit cards in my bag. He could steal what he wanted. So I pulled on a bathrobe and came out. He hadn't touched my handbag, and I felt pretty rotten for suspecting it. When he'd finished, he joked, 'If that's what happens when I'm late, I don't know what I'll get at my next drop-off.' We both laughed, and he left. I didn't worry that he'd come round again. It was a one-off and we both knew it.

I did finally meet my friend by the river, an hour late. She knew by my face I'd either met a new boyfriend and/or had sex. When I confessed, she cracked a joke about him having 'an appliance of science'. We still laugh about it now. But taking charge like that helped me get over David – and was a hell of a confidence boost.

Linda, 27

She confesses (boy–girl)

My personal trainer knew the meaning of a real workout

Louise wanted to get fit and find a new man. Tim's 'personal services' were just what she needed . . .

A personal trainer? For me? Not a chance. I could motivate myself perfectly well in the gym, thank you . . . when I found the time to go. Personal trainers were for the likes of Madonna, or rich and lazy people too embarrassed to use the gym on their own. Then my friend Marie hired one. Six months later, she was a changed woman – fit, positive and literally glowing. Landed herself a gorgeous man, too. She talked me into it. I didn't realise just how personal the training was going to get.

Marie's trainer sounded great, but he couldn't fit me in after work. I'd seen personal trainers in the gym at my health club, so I asked there. It was £40 an hour. Hmm. The flat needed redecorating, my wardrobe was seriously lacking in summer clothes, and a personal trainer felt like one luxury I could do without. But I hadn't had a boyfriend – or sex – for a year, I'd put on weight, and if I ended up like Marie, every penny would be worth it. So I signed up for a session with Tim.

I admit I was nervous. The thought of sweating away while some super-fit guy watched and/or bellowed at me to try harder didn't appeal at all. Nor did I want everyone in the gym thinking I was lazy or stuck-up. But without it, I knew I'd never get in shape. Lately I'd been to the gym once a month, and only then because my membership card stared at me once too often from my wallet.

The gym was busy, but I immediately noticed a hunk of a guy standing by the staff desk. I hadn't seen him before. Very short dark hair – almost shaved – with a tan and a chiselled, 'pretty' face. He was very fit, with huge arms practically bursting out of the staff T-shirt. If there's one thing I like, it's men with big arms and shoulders. Not too big – bodybuilders don't turn me on – but enough to get hold of. Then he turned round so his back was towards me and I saw the words 'personal trainer' on his T-shirt.

My first thought was, 'I hope that's not Tim.' I'd never be able to concentrate, let alone push myself, if he was watching over me. I didn't want him to see me sweaty, with no make-up. And I was wearing my oldest, grottiest tracksuit.

I asked for Tim. He said, 'Hi, you must be Louise.' When he smiled, my stomach did a somersault. Cute wasn't the word. His smile made me feel all fluttery inside. I hadn't fancied anyone this much for years.

Tim took me into a private room and asked about my health, my aims and level of fitness. I noticed his wedding ring. Then we went round looking at the equipment. He was very friendly, but his manner was always professional and businesslike. So was mine. He was married, and this was purely a working relationship.

It took me a while to relax with Tim. But by our fourth session, I was sweating and snorting my way round the gym with the best of them. I still fancied Tim, but at £40 an hour, I wanted to get fit. Then came the hottest day of the year – in more ways than one.

It was such a sunny day that I almost cancelled my gym session. Everyone was going down the pub, which sounded much more like it. But I went. The gym was almost empty. I told Tim I didn't feel motivated, so he suggested jogging by the river instead.

Being outside with Tim felt strange. He set the pace, but it was so hot that I had to sit down on a bench. Tim sat beside me. I tipped half a bottle of water over my head to cool down. Our eyes met – and that was it. I still don't know who made the first move. Suddenly we were kissing. Both of us were dripping wet. but I didn't care. His hand was on my breast, fingering my nipple through my bra. I was in ecstasy.

Tim whispered, 'D'you want to come back to my flat?' I replied, 'What about your wife?' He laughed. He wasn't married, but so many older women gave him the come-on at work that he wore the ring to put them off. I was his last client of the day, so we had plenty of time. When I said, 'OK, let's go,' he looked down at his shorts and said, 'We'd better wait a minute.' I realised he'd got a massive erection.

We walked to his flat with our arms round each other, stopping to kiss on the way. I couldn't get enough of him. Inside, he got us both a can of Diet Coke and said he was going for a shower.

The bathroom door wasn't locked. I couldn't resist going in. I took off my shorts and vest, poked my head around the shower curtain and said, 'Do you mind if I join you?'

It was the most sensual, yet explosive, sex I've ever had. As the hot water from the shower poured over us, we washed each other, starting at the shoulders and working down. Tim slid his soapy hand between my legs and I masturbated him too. It felt incredible. I knew I was going to come quickly, so I stopped masturbating him and concentrated on my own orgasm, rubbing myself against his hand. Tim was so turned on that he had to masturbate with his other hand. When he climaxed, I came, loud and hard.

We got dressed and Tim made a coffee, but I sensed he was waiting for me to leave. He didn't make much effort at conversation. Call me naive, but I'd honestly thought Tim was going to suggest a date.

I didn't feel used, because I was up for it too, and the sex was worth it. But I was disappointed. At our next session, Tim was his usual professional self, but I sensed a real distance between us. I didn't enjoy working out with him anymore, so I cancelled my sessions.

I still see Tim in the gym, and we acknowledge each other, but that's all. I've realised that most of his clients are older women, who book him again and again in the hope that one day they'll get a taste of his 'personal services'. I'm glad I did.

Louise, 27

She confesses (boy–girl)

Sex was our destiny

When clairvoyant Ally took a call from Michael, she sensed he wanted more than his fortune told . . .

His voice was the sexiest I've ever heard. Soft, gentle and with a faint Irish lilt. He wanted to book a consultation. I couldn't help flirting. He flirted back. I'd never dreamed of having sex with a client – it wasn't even a subconscious fantasy. But something about his voice had me hooked. Two hours later we were having amazing sex in my living room. I never did get to tell his fortune.

I suppose I should have seen it coming. I've worked as a self-employed clairvoyant for seven years. Trouble is, I never read my own cards. I don't want to know what the future has in store for me. My clients do. Most hear of me through word-of-mouth, but he'd seen my ad in the local paper. It's rare for a man to cold call, so I was surprised. He asked what type of fortune-telling I offered. Strictly cards – no ball-gazing. The innuendoes started from there. He sounded turned on by my voice, too. We flirted outrageously, and I heard myself arranging to give him a 'session' at 2 p.m.

When I put down the phone, I realised what I'd done. How did I feel? Sheer blind panic sums it up. Inviting a stranger into my house wasn't that unusual – new clients came to see me all the time, and my flatmate worked from home anyway. But this was a man, and we'd left each other in no doubt that we wanted sex. Was he a psychopath? What if I didn't fancy him? He sounded good-looking, but that didn't mean a thing. What if he wouldn't take 'no' for an answer? What if my boyfriend came round? What if my flatmate heard us? I hadn't even taken his phone number so I could cancel. Just as I decided to dial 1471, another client rang. It was too late to get his number. There was no way out.

I had a shower and decided he wouldn't turn up anyway. If he did, and I didn't fancy him, I'd pretend he'd got the wrong address. But the warmth of the shower relaxed me, and I masturbated. The whole idea excited me, and I reached orgasm quickly. Sex with my boyfriend had gone pretty stale. I'd never done anything like this before, and I might never get the chance again. So I put on my best underwear, a sexy camisole top and a short – but not too short – black skirt.

I told my flatmate that I had a consultation at 2 p.m., so she wouldn't disturb us, and watched out of the upstairs window. The bald, fat guy just couldn't be him. It wasn't. How about the student-looking guy on the push-bike? No, thank God. Then a car pulled up. Smart car, smart guy inside. Mid-thirties, casual clothes, chatting on a mobile phone. That couldn't be him. I couldn't be that lucky. Then he got out of the car and walked up my front path.

He was much better looking than I'd dared to hope. Short, dark hair, well over six foot and well-built – just how I like them. His eyes lit up when he saw me and I was sure he fancied me too. That was a relief. He said, 'Hi, are you Ally? I've got an appointment with you.' I nodded and led him into the living room. The cards were out on the table, just in case, but we didn't even pretend he wanted a consultation. He kissed me and we sat down on the sofa.

That afternoon was one of the most erotic experiences of my life. I felt like I'd stepped out of myself, as if it wasn't really me, and I was playing a role. I closed the curtains, locked the living-room door, and told him we'd need to keep quiet. My flatmate must have heard us. We licked, sucked, massaged, nibbled, played with an ice cube, gave each other oral sex and even blindfolded each other with my silk scarf. He was very, very skilled, stopping me just before I came, which totally heightened the feeling. He reached orgasm three times – twice as I gave him oral sex, and once inside me. I didn't want to come too soon, but after his third orgasm, he went down on me and I couldn't hold back. My flatmate must have heard that one!

He wanted to carry on, but I'd had an intense orgasm and, to be honest, I wanted him to leave. I'm sure he didn't want a relationship either – this was strictly a one-off. We'd met for sex and we'd had it. I whispered I'd got another appointment, so we'd better get dressed. He was cool about it. I didn't ask for his number, and as he left he said, 'Maybe we'll meet again,' but I knew he didn't mean it. He never called.

I still can't believe I did it. I'll never know if he makes a habit of it – or if he really wanted his fortune told. I'd guess the latter – he was too good-looking to need to pick up women that way. My flatmate never said a word, but she gave me a knowing wink. When my boyfriend came round that night, I was so horny that we had full-on sex all evening. It definitely spiced up our sex life – but I wouldn't take a risk like that again. I know I got very, very lucky.

Ally, 29

He confesses (boy–girl)

I had sex with my driving instructor

Tim was looking forward to his driving lessons, but he didn't realise steamy windows were about to become more than just a fantasy . . .

I'm into uniforms. She wasn't wearing one, of course, But she looked smart, businesslike, in charge. Prim and proper. That was good enough for me. I wanted sex from the moment I saw her. But I didn't think I'd get it.

We met in the foyer of the driving school. My first lesson. Five-day crash course. Embarrassing enough being 28 and a non-driver. Thought they'd give me a nice old codger. The 'surrogate dad' type. That would have been fine by me. Then Katie came over.

She was tall. Very tall. Legs that went on forever. Huge eyes. Long dark hair, tied back. Late twenties, at a guess. No wedding ring. No uniform either, but she had a sexy air of confidence, authority. She turned me on without even trying. For a split second, I couldn't believe my luck. Then I panicked.

I could handle it on planes. Happened all the time when I looked at female flight attendants. Still does. Something about women in authority . . .

Sure, my ex-girlfriends had dressed up for me. I even dated a flight attendant for a while. We had amazing sex every time she got in from work. This was different. Just me and Katie. In the car for an hour, inches apart. I felt about fourteen and worried I'd look like a total prat and/or get an erection.

Every time I looked at her, I imagined her stripping off. So I stopped looking and focused on the driving instead. She was polite, calm and a damn good instructor. No chit-chat. I told the lads I'd got a female instructor and laughed along at the 'woman driver' jokes. When I had sex with my girlfriend that night, Katie was my fantasy.

She didn't give off any sexual vibes at all – until the second lesson. I got stuck in gear and she put her hand on mine to move the gear stick. I felt myself getting hard. Like I was going to explode. I looked across at her legs, which made me even harder. I had a baggy T-shirt on to hide it. We caught each other's eye. She giggled like a little kid. The confident, businesslike mask slipped, just for a moment. She fancied me too.

If we'd been in the pub, I'd have flirted, no problem. You might think being cooped up in the car was the perfect set-up. She couldn't get away. That's what scared me. There was no way she'd make the first move – her job was at stake. What if I made a dick of myself – or, even worse, she accused me of sexual harassment?

It happened at the end of the last lesson. I was her last client each day that week. As usual, she asked if she could drop me anywhere on her way home. I suggested a pub. Said I was meeting some mates.

The car park was busy, but she pulled into a space. I asked if she fancied a drink. She took off her seat-belt, smiled, and said, 'Let's not bother with that.' Then she leaned across and kissed me. I couldn't believe my luck. Talk about 'in charge' . . .

We kissed for ages. I reached inside her top and stroked her breasts. She undid my jeans and masturbated me. The car was completely steamed up, but I didn't care if anyone saw us. My fantasy was coming true. She bent over and gave me oral sex. I pulled the comb out of her hair and it fell down, loose, all over my lap. The sight of her hair, and her head moving up and down, and the amazing way she flicked my penis with her tongue, meant I couldn't hold back, and I orgasmed.

She sat up and I reached across to masturbate her. But she tilted her seat back, opened her legs and pulled my head towards her. I gave her oral sex. She slid her finger down to her clitoris and helped me bring her to orgasm.

We sat up and I offered her a cigarette, which we shared in silence. I didn't know what the hell to do. What if someone had seen us and my girlfriend had found out? I'd had an incredible orgasm, lived out a fantasy, but now it was over. I couldn't get out of the car like some heartless bastard, but I didn't want to go for a drink with her either.

Then she said, 'It just happened, OK. Don't tell anyone or I'll be in the shit.' Thank God. It was a one-off for her, too. That got me off the hook. I said, 'Sure, no problem. I'd better let you go, then,' and got out of the car. She opened my window and I said, 'That was fantastic.' She smiled and drove off.

I still fantasise about that blow-job. It was the best I've ever had. Never thought I'd hear myself say it, but it was better than full sex. Oh, and I passed my driving test too.

Tim, 28

He confesses (boy–girl)

She seduced me on her dentist's chair

Graham was terrified of the drill – until he was alone with his sexy new dentist . . .

I hated dentists. OK, I admit it, I was terrified. Phobic, even. If I ever wanted to stop myself coming too soon, thinking about dentists always did the trick. A far better show-stopper than the Inland Revenue. So the last person I expected to fancy was my dentist – and the last place I thought I'd have sex was in the dreaded chair.

Put me in a board meeting, a job interview, even a high-pressure pitch for a major new client (I'm an ad executive), and I am fine. Nervous and keyed-up, but fine. But if you sat me in a waiting room with that smell and high-pitched drilling, I lose it and have to dash out for 'an important appointment'. The upshot was I hadn't been to the dentist for years. So I got toothache. Serious toothache. The kind that keeps you awake at night. My fantasies changed from Pamela Anderson to pulling out the offending tooth with pliers. Sex – and masturbating – were totally out of the question. I had to do something. A friend told me her female dentist specialised in 'nervous patients', so after three weeks of suffering and Nurofen Plus, I booked myself an appointment.

I sat sweating in the waiting room for the longest ten minutes of my life. It was only the constant throbbing in my jaw that kept me there. Then the door opened and the dentist walked out. Short, dark hair, big dark eyes and a pretty smile. I noticed she was attractive, but I was in no fit mental state to think about it. She called out my name and I followed her into the room.

Somehow she managed to put me at ease. Her whole manner was calm and caring. She said she saw a lot of nervous patients and if I felt anxious, all I had to do was tell her and we'd stop for a bit. I sat down in the dreaded chair and she tipped me backwards. That's when I saw her face up close, just before she put the mask on. Her eyes were huge, deep brown – and gorgeous. Even though all she did was have a look and give me a prescription for antibiotics, I left feeling proud of myself.

By my third visit, I was relaxed enough to stop worrying and start noticing how sexy she was. Don't get me wrong – she was always totally professional, and I was still too nervous to get an erection in the chair. But there was something about the way she smiled that convinced me she fancied me too. When I masturbated, it was often her in my mind.

The lads at work said I should ask her out. Sounded like a bad idea to me. What if she was married? She didn't wear a ring, but maybe she couldn't in her job. If she turned me down, I'd feel a right prat. And I'd never get my teeth sorted . . .

Three months – and many fantasies – later, I plucked up courage and asked her. It was my last appointment for six months. As I got my coat, the dental nurse went out of the room. It was now or never. I said, 'I've got a spare ticket for the cinema tonight. Would you like it?' She smiled and said, 'Are you going too?' I knew I was in business.

We met outside the cinema, but we didn't bother with the film. I took her out for dinner and we talked all night. She looked gorgeous in a low-cut top and jeans. I'd only ever seen her in a white overall. When someone's drilled around inside your mouth, you feel pretty intimate already. She stayed the night at my flat, but we didn't stop talking until dawn. We fell asleep on the sofa, and when I woke up, she'd undone my shirt and was kissing my chest. I moved to touch her too, but she said, 'Lie back and enjoy it.'

She kissed and licked all over my chest. I was so horny I reached down and undid my trousers. As I masturbated, she put her hand over mine and felt how I did it. Then I took my hand away and she carried on. Her touch was perfect, not too soft, not too heavy. I didn't want to come too soon – and thinking about dentists wasn't going to work this time – so I rolled her on to her back and kissed her breasts. She was masturbating through her jeans, so I slid them down and put my hand over hers, so I could feel how she touched herself. As she touched herself, I slipped my finger inside her, and I felt her whole body shudder as she orgasmed. I couldn't hold back, so I quickly brought myself to orgasm too. A cup of coffee and some TV later, we had full sex all over the bed and the bedroom floor.

We dated regularly after that, and I switched to another dentist at the practice. She didn't want to be accused of dating a client. One night, I met her at the surgery. She was finishing some paperwork, so I sat in the dreaded chair to wait. Everyone else had gone home.

She started it. I was lying right back, staring at the ceiling, when the lights went out. I felt her hand sliding up my leg. I jumped, but she whispered, 'It's OK', slid her hand between my legs and stroked my balls. I went hard. She stripped slowly. Then she undid my jeans, stood astride me and moved slowly up and down on my penis. I masturbated her, and she moved faster and faster. The feeling was so intense, we both came hard and quick. Afterwards, we both laughed and she said, 'I've always wanted to do that.'

Our relationship lasted a year, but we're still friends and I still go to the same dental practice. Whenever I sit in the chair, I think about what we did in it.

Graham, 30

She confesses (boy–girl)

My window cleaner whet my sexual appetite

Mel saw him through the bedroom window and knew she had to have him . . .

OK, I admit it. I've fantasised about him. The window cleaner in the Diet Coke ad. You know the guy. All suntan and muscles. Knows what to do and has the body to do it. Just a touch of sweat – enough to look turned on and ready for sex. I wanted him to climb through my window and push me back on the bed. Rough, raw sex, with no names, no commitments. But my window cleaner was more Newcastle Brown Ale than Diet Coke. Surely my fantasy would never come true . . .

Reg cleaned the windows every other Thursday. Puce, pot-bellied, mid-forties. Builder's bottom on the ladder, let alone when he bent over his bucket. But reliable. I was late for work when I heard the van pull up, so I dashed out of the front door, clutching the £12 I owed him.

It wasn't Reg. This guy was straight out of my fantasy. Very tall, very big build, very blonde and very tanned. Bit young, early twenties, but I didn't care. Wearing 501s, topless, with a white T-shirt hanging loose from his front pocket. He lifted a ladder from the top of the van. That body really turned me on. I had to have him. Maybe not now, but sometime soon. Very soon. Just once.

I wished he could stay nameless, but I was already walking towards him. I had to stop and chat. He had bright blue eyes and a cute beauty spot above his top lip. A decent voice, too – well-spoken. Not that it mattered. His name was Dave, he was 24, and had taken over from Reg. I couldn't believe my luck.

I changed my shifts so I was home every other Thursday morning. Luckily, Dave turned up after my boyfriend had gone to work. It was a long, hot summer. We joked and flirted, sometimes for half an hour. The usual innuendoes, the touch on the shoulder. Nothing happened. I found out he was single. When I had sex with my boyfriend, I fantasised about Dave.

I wanted Dave to make the first move. That was my fantasy. I knew he fancied me, so I would sit in the garden in my sexiest swimsuit. I would follow him from room to room as he cleaned, smiling seductively through the windows. He would grin back. Still nothing.

Then, one Thursday, he didn't turn up. By lunchtime, I was completely wound up and frustrated. I knew I was being ridiculous, but the chance of sex with Dave, of fulfilling my fantasy, was like a drug. Then I saw his van. It couldn't go on any longer. He put his ladder up to the spare bedroom window and started work.

I'd had enough of playing games. I wanted sex with him so badly that I felt I had nothing to lose. If he wouldn't make the first move, I would. I went up to the spare bedroom. He waved at me through the window and carried on cleaning. I made eye contact with him and held it while I took off my sandals. Then I peeled off my T-shirt. I was pretty nervous, but deep down I felt sure he wanted me too.

Dave stared through the window in disbelief. He could not take his eyes off me. This was different from my fantasy, but the feeling of power and control turned me on even more. I stopped feeling nervous and started enjoying it. I slid out of my skirt and pulled down my knickers. Dave's mouth had literally dropped open.

I thought about masturbating, but instead I walked to the window, opened it and said, 'Do you fancy me?' He replied, 'What do you think?' I looked down at the enormous bulge in his jeans and grinned. I said, 'Can you be discreet?' and he nodded. In my fantasy, he climbed through the window, but in reality it looked pretty dangerous, so I pulled on a dressing gown and said I'd let him in through the front door.

He asked if my boyfriend would be coming back. I shook my head and double-locked the front door. 'He can't get in,' I told him. 'If he does, you can pretend to clean the windows.' We both giggled.

I led him up to the spare bedroom. He was very nervous – not the strong, silent type of my fantasy at all. But it didn't matter. I took the lead and enjoyed it. I unzipped his jeans. His hands were shaking. Then we kissed. Passion took over and he wasn't nervous at all.

Dave knew exactly how to touch me. I was so turned on by the situation anyway that I came very quickly. Then we made love in every position you can imagine. When he finally orgasmed, I came again. It was the most intense, exciting sexual experience of my life.

Even though I'd made it happen, I felt very embarrassed afterwards. I'd taken a huge risk – I didn't really know Dave at all. I just wanted him to go. Dave was stroking me and talking about 'next time'. I didn't want a next time. He knew I lived with my boyfriend. Nice house, car, lifestyle – he'd seen it all. I thought he understood this was a one-off.

I went for a shower. Dave had got dressed but he was still sitting on the bed. I cringed. He asked why I'd 'gone all cold' on him. I felt awful. Eventually I said I'd think about seeing him again, just to get him out of the house.

I rang the window-cleaning company and cancelled my contract. Two weeks later, I went to work all day on Thursday to avoid him. But I got home to find him cleaning my neighbour's windows. We said a polite 'hello' but he followed me up the path and asked if we could talk. It was creepy. I told him no, politely but firmly, and shut the door. After that, I stayed away from the house on Thursdays. Reg is back doing the rounds now. I haven't seen Dave since.

Sex with my window cleaner was the most amazing sexual

experience of my life, and I often fantasise about it. I wish we'd been able to say 'goodbye and thanks' as friends. At least I know he enjoyed it as much as I did.

Mel, 29

He confesses (boy–girl)

She brought out the animal in me

Andrew hated looking after his friend's cat, until the day he took it to the vet . . .

Thank God for Trude Mostue. It wasn't her, of course – I didn't get that lucky. But she's living proof that vets can be very, very sexy. Before Trude, vets weren't exactly up there with female lifeguards, models and Daryl Hannah (my personal favourite). Not with the lads in my pub, anyway. But they are now . . .

I've got Mike to thank for it. Dumping his cat with me. Mike does a great line in 'We're leaving for the airport in two hours and I've forgotten to book the bloody cattery . . . She'll kill me. Go on, mate; it's only for two weeks . . .' Happens every time. I hate the sodding cat, too. Big, fluffy and looks exactly like Mike's live-in girlfriend, who fusses over it like it's a baby. But this time, putting up with Fluffy led to the hottest sex I've ever had.

I'd been single for almost a year. Sure, I'd had a few one-night stands. Lots of sexual build-up, then a quick drunken session at the end of it. Sometimes I even stayed for breakfast. But I never got past that, never met anyone who made me want to take it further – until my unscheduled trip to the vet's. The last place on earth you expect to find the world's best blow-job.

Mike's girlfriend had left me instructions, of course – which food, which milk, what time, even the vet's name and phone number. Straight in the bin with that. In my flat, it's a tin of Spar's finest whenever I roll in from the pub. So five days into my cat-sitting, when the cat wasn't well, I panicked. Could I remember the vet's name? No chance. A quick shufti through the *Yellow Pages* and I'd found a veterinary practice around the corner. Seven o'clock that night with 'Miss Smith'. She'd do.

The waiting room was empty. Then she opened the door. Talk about stereotypes – I was expecting a big, beefy spinster. But she was late twenties and stunning, even with the white coat. Long dark hair, tied back, a toothpaste-ad smile and huge brown eyes. Tanned, too – she'd definitely been away somewhere. Not many women can leave me lost for words, but she was one of them. I lugged the cat basket into the consulting room and mumbled about him being 'not well'.

She lifted Fluffy out of the basket and checked him over, talking to him in a gorgeous, gentle voice. I couldn't stop staring at her. Even her hands, her long, tanned fingers, were sexy. She wasn't wearing a wedding ring – but then, she wasn't wearing any rings at all. Probably had to take them off, I decided. Someone like her was bound to be married.

I wish I could say the chemistry was electric. It was on my side, but she was totally professional. I didn't pick up any vibes at all. I left the surgery forty quid lighter, with a bag-load of tablets and a very cross cat. I'd fancied girls before, but this was something else. I went straight home to masturbate.

Five days of walking past the surgery finally paid off. We literally bumped into each other. She recognised me straight away. I was in with a chance. When she remembered the cat's name, I knew at least one of us had made an impression. I'd masturbated over her endlessly, but I still felt sexually frustrated. I wanted *her*. All my well-rehearsed lines evaporated and I heard myself saying, 'Do you fancy a drink?' It sounded cheesy and I thought I'd blown it, but she replied, 'Sure? Now?'

We went to the pub opposite. Turned out she was single too – her boyfriend had finished with her six months before. What kind of idiot was he? Working long hours meant she hardly ever met anyone, and inviting clients out for a drink was off limits. Now I did feel sexual vibes, and lots of them. She wanted me. She was sexually frustrated too. Her hand kept touching mine as we talked. By the fourth drink, I was feeling brave. Did she want to come back to my place? She did.

I thought we'd have a bottle of wine, chat some more, then I'd make my move. But she took charge the moment we were inside my front door. As I closed it, she put her arms around me and kissed me hard. Our hands were everywhere. I felt her tugging at my jeans, then she slid down and gave me oral sex right there on the doormat. The neighbours across the corridor must have heard us, but I didn't care.

I looked down to watch, which gave me a real kick. She was masturbating herself furiously. The sight of her masturbating turned me on and I knew I was going to come, so I tried to pull back, but she wouldn't let me go. I felt her coming, and my orgasm was just explosive. It was by far the best blow-job I've ever had.

I'd be lying if I said there wasn't an awkward pause. She was embarrassed and so was I. I'll never forget her words – she said, 'Sorry – I needed that.' I told her it was definitely not something to apologise about! Now it was my turn to take charge. This was my flat, and I should make her feel at home. I got us both a drink, lit the fire and put the TV on so we weren't pressured to talk. The cat jumped straight on her lap. By the second glass of wine, we were kissing, and ended up having full sex, with her on top, on the sofa.

I thought she'd stay the night, but I came to around 2 a.m., still on the sofa, and she was phoning for a cab. I asked for her number. She said she'd had a great night, but she wasn't ready for a relationship and hoped we'd see each other around. I was disappointed, but when I thought about it afterwards, we didn't have much in common. She was into opera and films with subtitles – I'm a Rolling Stones and *Die Hard* man myself. It was just sex.

When Mike came home, I told him I'd had an amazing session with the vet. He was dumbstruck. 'But he's an old geezer . . .' he said. I told him that it was time to change his vet's practice.

Andrew, 25

5
Start at the Top

Sex with the boss doesn't always land you in hot water – our saucy readers can vouch for that. But why stop there, when you can have a sex-tastic session with the boss's wife, boss's daughter – or even your boyfriend's boss . . .

One raunchy reader figured a well-timed blow-job was bound to earn her that promotion. And Simon took his role of 'right-hand man' a little too literally at the office party. Find out what happens when our confessors rub shoulders – and bodies – with the top brass.

She confesses (girl–girl)

I had a lesbian fling with my boss's wife

Lisa hated her boss's domineering wife Anna – until she got to know her much more intimately . . .

Anna didn't just drop into the office. She always made a big entrance, sweeping in with a huge billowing coat that cost more than my monthly salary. We didn't even get a 'hello'. She went straight past us underlings into Andrew's office. He was lucky if she bothered to knock. It was his firm, and she was his wife, so I guess she could damn well do as she pleased. But treating us like dirt ensured every woman in the company loathed her. So Anna was the last person on earth I expected to have sex with.

I admit it, I fancied her. Even her ghastly personality didn't

94

override her looks. She reminded me of Nelle in *Ally McBeal*. Long, curly blonde hair, a gorgeous figure draped in thousands of pounds' worth of clothes, and steel grey eyes. Anna wasn't like us. She didn't go to the gym when she put on weight or when the unused membership card made her feel guilty once too often. The gym was her life. Once she even came in wearing a tennis skirt. That really turned me on. But I never dreamed anything would happen. For a start, I didn't even like her.

On the rare occasions when she did glance at you, the vibe was totally, 'Don't mess with me'. But when she looked at me, I sensed something more. She couldn't hold eye contact. I don't advertise the fact I'm bisexual, but I don't hide it either. Andrew definitely knew, so you can bet your life he'd told Anna. My sexuality definitely unnerved her. I couldn't decide if it turned her on or off – until our summer 'outing'.

Every year, Andrew organised a day-trip to the seaside for all the staff. It was better than a day in the office, but it always took the same form. Everyone got horribly drunk outside the same pub on the seafront, pigged out on fish and chips and felt rough on the train home. The difference this year was that Anna was coming. When Andrew told us, we groaned inwardly. But she turned out to be quite a laugh, especially after a few drinks. All those designer clothes and that attitude were her armour against what she saw as an office full of bitchy women.

I ended up sitting next to her outside the pub. We had a great chat. I was amazed to find out she had a degree – though I didn't show it – and I couldn't take my eyes off her breasts. I tried not to show that either. She was wearing a beautiful girlie dress. It was blazing hot and her hair was shining white in the sun. I wanted her more than I've ever wanted any woman, but I didn't dare make any kind of move. Even flirting was out. If anyone noticed, we'd be gossiped about for years.

People drifted off to do their own thing, leaving Anna, Andrew, another guy – Simon – and me. We'd got a couple of hours before the train home. Suddenly Anna piped up, 'Lisa, will you come shopping with me? You don't mind, do you Andrew?' He was happy to stay in the pub. So was Simon, playing his cards for promotion. So we wandered towards the town centre.

Anna was giggly and very nervous. I asked if she was OK. Then she said, 'I'll probably regret saying this for ever, but do you want to check into a hotel for a couple of hours?'

There aren't many situations that leave me lost for words, but that was one of them. She looked really embarrassed and said, 'Oh, sorry, look, just forget I ever said anything, OK?' I grabbed her hand and said: 'No, I'd love to. Are you sure?'

She went straight back into 'Anna' mode, sweeping into a very grand-looking hotel and booking a room on her credit card. We giggled all the way up in the lift. When we got in the room, we fell onto the bed, still laughing, and Anna said, 'I've never done this before. You won't tell anyone, will you?' She looked excited and scared. So was I.

I took the lead, kissing her gently all over and slipping down her dress. She stroked and kissed me. I was desperate to touch her clitoris, but aware it was her first time, I knew I had to take it slowly. When I did touch her, she let out an incredible, deep groan of pleasure. I quickly masturbated her to orgasm. She came very hard. Then she said, 'I don't know how to touch you,' so I took her hand and helped her bring me to orgasm.

I'll never forget lying on that bed, in the sun, with Anna curled up in my arms. We had sex once more. This time, it was wilder. Anna felt more confident and we gave each other the sweetest oral sex until we both came. When we left, she said, 'That was amazing.'

We were so worried about missing the train that we turned up first at the station. Watching her go back to Andrew didn't hurt – I hadn't even contemplated a relationship. I felt sure Anna was straight. This was a one-off. Afterwards, I did worry she'd tell him, or he'd see her credit card slip, or somehow find out and it would affect my job, but he never did. I kept my word and didn't tell a soul. Giving me the come-on was a brave thing to do in her position, and I respected her for that. Anna still swept into the office, though I always got a 'hello' and a big grin. I switched firms a few months later, so I never did find out if she wanted a repeat performance on the next summer trip.

Lisa, 26

He confesses (boy–girl)

I was seduced by my boss

Tom thought his boss was out of reach – until she showed him the true meaning of 'a job well done' . . .

She was blonde, bubbly and very, very shrewd. *Big Brother*'s Helen with a degree in management. One hell of a business brain and a lot of charm. Everyone loved her, but she was the boss. A laugh and a joke in the pub were fine. Chat about sex and she'd giggle along. A little flirting was OK, too, but get too personal, and the shutters came down. Her home life was strictly off limits. So when I offered her a lift home, I was expecting a friendly chat – not sex in the front seat.

Talk about assertive. Come first, think later. I didn't have a chance to say no – not that I would have, of course. Not many guys would turn down a blow-job from Jo. Not straight ones, anyway. One minute I was doing up my seat-belt, the next her head was in my lap and I was – shall we say – rising to the occasion. Big time. And reliving it every day for months afterwards. Two years on, I still fantasise about it.

I'd worked at the hairdressing salon for six months. Jo hired me. There were six stylists plus Jo, and our working relationships were all slightly flirty. Good salons are always like that. Flirting gives the place a buzz. Everyone knows it isn't serious. Jo, being the boss, flirted the least, but she was so bubbly and upbeat that she made the salon a great place to work.

I admit I fancied her like crazy. So did the other male stylists. None of us thought we stood a chance – and that made her even more attractive. Flirting with her felt safe because it couldn't possibly lead anywhere. That didn't stop me masturbating over thoughts of her, though. Even Paul, who was gay, could see why men fell for her. Women loved her, too. Male clients just wanted to be with her, female clients wanted to *be* her. Every one kept coming back. The salon's takings were huge compared to anywhere else I'd worked. We all deserved some credit for that but, if I'm honest, it was largely down to Jo.

Her boyfriend drove a Porsche – lucky sod – and often picked her up from the salon. I didn't like him. He was the classic City-boy type – all suit, smart car and sneer. Us stylists were clearly an inferior race, though I bet he never pulled that attitude on Jo. She'd have eaten him alive. God knows what she saw in him, apart from a big wallet. None of us – even the girls – could work it out.

The night it happened – and this made it totally perfect – his brand-new Porsche broke down. Jo and I were the last two people left in the salon. She was waiting for him, and I was killing time before meeting my latest girlfriend outside the cinema. Then Jo's mobile rang. He was stuck on 'the bloody Marylebone Road'. The thought of him being hooted and yelled at for holding up the traffic just made my day. Jo said she'd get a cab to his place. I offered to drive her. Why not? I had another hour to kill and it was only ten minutes away.

I know what you're thinking – I wanted to get her in my car

and seduce her. Totally wrong. Seducing Jo was the last thing on my mind. Anyway, she isn't the kind of girl you *can* seduce. When Jo sees something she wants, she just goes for it. I didn't think I was on her 'most wanted' list. . .

Jo suggested grabbing a quick drink at the pub opposite. That wasn't unusual – we often drank there. But when we sat down at a table outside, I realised this was the first time we'd ever been alone. Jo was her bubbly self, but she was flirting far more than usual. When we looked at each other, I sensed she was giving me one hell of a come-on. With anyone else, I'd have gone for it straight away, but I couldn't quite believe that Jo was serious. We were meeting our partners in less than an hour and she was my boss. This had nowhere to go. That wouldn't normally bother me, but I didn't want to misread the situation and end up looking stupid. Still, it was fun so I flirted back. By the time we finished our second drink, the sexual tension was incredible. She was wearing this cute halter-neck top and I'd been marvelling at her breasts all day. Now they were right in front of me, willing me to touch them.

Jo said we'd better go, so we went round the back of the salon to my car. I unlocked her door and said something about it not being up to her usual Porsche standards. As I got in my seat, Jo said, 'The car might not be, but I'll bet you are.' She leaned across the handbrake and kissed me.

I didn't care about my girlfriend, her City bloke, the fact it was still broad daylight, or that we'd probably never be able to face each other again. She kissed me all the way down to my penis, unzipped my jeans and gave me the most incredible blow-job I've ever had.

It sounds selfish, and I didn't mean to be, but I was so overcome by the whole thing that I just sat there unable to move, unable to do anything except feel her bringing me closer and closer to orgasm. I came with a torrent of sexy swear words. She sat up and kissed me again. Even though I'd come, we were still full-on. I stroked and kissed her breasts, but she grabbed my hand and pushed it up her skirt, so I masturbated her roughly. She liked that. Then she pulled what looked like a lipstick out of her pocket, giggled and said, 'Use this.' It was a mini vibrator. I rested it on her clitoris, with one finger inside her. She writhed about on the seat, got very, very wet and came hard and quickly.

We carried on kissing, and I tried to turn the vibrator off with one hand, but I couldn't. It wouldn't stop buzzing, and we both laughed. Jo said, 'For God's sake, swat that fly.' I twisted it off, and handed it back to Jo. She said, 'Now you know what I get up to when I'm in the loo.' Then she checked her watch and said: 'God, you'd better drop me off. You'll miss your film.' It was so typically Jo. Back to business.

I drove to her boyfriend's house in a weird state of ecstasy and paranoia. What we'd just done was incredible, the best, but where did it leave us? Would her boyfriend somehow know and emerge from his front door with a machete?

I'd have dated Jo in a second if she'd suggested it. But she didn't. His Porsche still wasn't home, but she kissed me on the cheek, said, 'I've just always wanted to do that. I hope we can keep it to ourselves, OK?' and got out of the car. I met my girlfriend – slightly late – and sat through the film with a massive hard-on as I relived those ten minutes in the car. Did I have sex with my girlfriend afterwards? What do you think? We had a hot, sticky, all-night session – and at one point she asked what had got me so worked up. I lied.

I stayed at the salon for another year, and I resisted the urge to tell the lads at work what we'd done – though I did tell them after I left. Part of me was dreading finding out that she'd done it with one – or all – of them, but she hadn't. No one noticed anything between me and Jo, but when we looked at each other, that raw desire was still there. For her, this was all about sex, nothing more, and I accepted that. Maybe the City boy didn't satisfy her. Maybe she just fancied sex with me too. I'll never know the reason.

We did have sex twice more – once in the car, when I gave her a lift home after someone's birthday party, and once in the loo. She was working late and I found an excuse to hang around. She pulled out her lipstick vibrator, said, 'You're good with these,' and I ended up having sex with her from behind over one of the wash-basins. But that's another story . . .

Tom, 25

He confesses (boy–girl)

I had sex with the boss's daughter

Andy thought Jade was perfect – until he found out who she was . . .

Every guy you'll ever meet has a treasured possession. Mine's my BMW. Mark, my best mate, loves his Fender guitar. Our managing director adores his daughter, Jade. The one rule with treasured possessions is look, admire, desire – but never touch. So what did I do? Broke the rule big time by having hot, sweaty sex with Jade at the firm's Christmas party.

Don't blame me – I had no idea who she was. Our MD is in his late forties, one of the lads, dynamic, divorced because he's married to the job, and the last person you'd expect to have a stunning twenty-something daughter. I knew he had two kids, but judging by the couple of photos on his desk, they were much younger. I'd never seen them, or his ex-wife, but he had a very horny blonde girlfriend who'd starred in the fantasies of almost every guy in the office. Especially mine. When she arrived at the party with Jade, I thought they were mates. Maybe even sisters.

I'd worked at the architectural firm for over a year, so I knew the Christmas party form. Take over a local restaurant for lunch, then down the pub until closing. Pretty good, as parties go, and far better than some organised 'do'. Jade turned up in the pub, so we were already drunk. I noticed her straight away. So did every other guy in the place. She was even more stunning than Joanne, the boss's girlfriend – thin, pretty and very, very cute.

My mate Mark was over there like a shot. He's irrepressible, totally full-on. What he lacks in looks, he makes up for in personality. The trouble is, women usually want him as their best friend – while Mark wants sex. I drifted round to talk to the guys in accounts and left Mark to get on with it. To be honest, I didn't think Mark, I, or anyone else from the firm, stood a chance with her.

The bar was packed, and when I went up to get a round in, I found myself squashed right next to her. I came out with some truly terrible line, like, 'Crowded here, isn't it?' but it got us chatting. She was 21, at uni and training to be a vet. I asked how she knew Joanne, and she replied, 'Oh, she's a friend of my dad's.'

Call me thick, call me stupid, but the penny didn't drop. I'd also had the best part of six pints of lager. Looking back, she assumed I knew who she was. I noticed the MD looking over at me a few times and – this is a real classic – I *smiled* at him, as if to say, 'I'm *in* here.'

Mark was standing further along the bar, trying to catch my eye. I deliberately didn't look at him. All he wanted to do, I figured, was give me the thumbs-up or mouth 'you lucky bastard'. Of course, what he really wanted to do was tell me that Jade was the MD's daughter.

Jade wasn't drunk but she was very flirty. I was totally bowled over, and amazed she was interested in me. She had the cutest breasts I'd ever seen – small but perfect, and when she caught me staring at them, she licked her lips slowly and ran her fingers up and down the outside of my leg. I went so hard that I put my hand in my pocket to try to hide my erection, though we were so squashed that no one would have noticed. Jade did. She slid her hand over my penis and gave it a squeeze. I let out a moan. Then she said, 'Come on, let's get out of here.'

We pushed through the crowd and crashed through the double doors into the street. It was freezing outside, and she was only wearing a dress, so I put my arm around her. She led me down a side street and unlocked a brand-new Peugeot 106, saying, 'I'm the driver tonight. They didn't want to get a cab.'

We climbed in the back seat. Jade pulled a blanket off the parcel shelf and we huddled under it like a couple of kids, giggling. Then she kissed me. I couldn't keep my hands off her, especially her breasts. I licked and massaged them. She pushed my head between her legs – she was obviously one of those girls who know what they want and are used to getting it – and I gave her oral sex under the blanket, using my fingers too. Jade arched her back and I knew she was going to come. I had to masturbate – I couldn't wait any longer, and I came within seconds of her.

I sat up, and found myself apologising for making a bit of a mess on the back seat. She giggled, grabbed a box of tissues from the front and said, 'You'd better clean it up before my dad gets in later.' I said, 'Is your dad here, at the party?' Jade looked incredulous. She said, 'Don't you know?' I shook my head. 'It's my dad's firm. He's the MD.'

Trust me, no matter how good sex with Jade was, it wasn't worth that feeling of total horror. I thought I was going to throw up. I said, 'Oh my God. He's going to kill me.' Jade just laughed and said: 'He won't know, because I won't tell him, and you won't. This is between us, OK? By the way, that was one hell of a blow-job.' She confessed to coming to the party feeling horny and hoping for a quickie, but most guys she'd chatted to had run a mile. I knew why.

I kissed her goodbye and got out of the car, praying word wouldn't get out – the boss always heard all the gossip. Telling Steve was out of the question – the entire office would know within minutes. The thought of going back to the pub was too much, so I went straight to the bus-stop, not even going back for my coat.

I spent the weekend dreading Monday, and getting alternately turned on and terrified by what we'd done in the car. Did I feel used? Maybe a bit, but hell, who cares? And she genuinely thought I knew who she was.

Steve was already at his desk when I arrived. I told him I went home after throwing up, and casually asked for the party gossip. There was plenty of it, but I could tell by his face that Steve didn't know my secret. Now it was down to the MD.

He breezed past my desk as usual, grinned and said, 'I hear you weren't too well at the party. My daughter said she was going to take you home until you threw up in the back of her car. Can't take your drink, eh, Andy?'

If only he knew . . .

Andy, 27

She confesses (boy-girl)

I had sex with my boss to get a pay rise

Sally hoped a leg-over would earn her a leg up . . .

Monica Lewinsky – I've got some sympathy for you, hon. Telling the *Cosmo* girls about this is embarrassing enough, but at least I can do it in secret. I honestly thought that giving the boss a well-timed blow-job would lick the opposition and land me that extra £6,000 a year as a senior sales manager. Enough to pay for a posh health club membership and stop me hyperventilating with guilt every time I blew £500 in Monsoon. That had to be worth it. So I followed Mr Jones into the boardroom and played my master stroke . . .

The weirdest part was how easy it was. He wasn't some overweight, balding 50-year-old. Steve Jones was in his early forties, married with kids – yes, I admit I knew, totally unforgivable – and good-looking in a Steve Martin way. Nice body, cute smile, grey hair but lots of it. He didn't flirt, ever. Steve had been on so many management training courses that he was the archetypal company man – 'correct' from his body language and punctuality to his expensive, well-cut suit. But I'd seen a spark in his bright blue eyes when he interviewed me. No management training course can hide that. I knew Steve wanted me.

I've always been ambitious. I want to win. Make that 'have to'. Board games, sports, work projects – I have to be the best. I'd been working with Steve for over a year when my direct boss left. I wanted that job. So did two other managers in my department. There would be a board interview, but Steve, as group manager, would hold sway. I worked long hours and generally behaved as if the job was already mine. Steve dropped a few hints about what to say at the interview, how to impress the board. But I had to be sure they'd choose me . . .

Maybe it was the way he held eye contact with me that little bit too long. Maybe it was because he seemed slightly jittery around me. I sensed a sexual vibe and, when it came to that promotion, I'm ashamed to say I was determined to use it. I guess it serves me right that the whole plan backfired . . .

My best friend Ceri warned me I'd end up the loser. She was so full of 'what ifs' that I wondered how the hell she ever made a decision. It seemed perfectly straightforward to me. I had it all planned out. I'd give Steve the come-on, get him back to my place, have sex, and then he'd be so worried I'd tell his wife that he'd give me the job just to shut me up. I wouldn't tell her, of course – I didn't want to split up a family. But he didn't know that. The way I saw it, I deserved the bloody job anyway. I wasn't jumping over better candidates. This was just an insurance policy.

I chose a week when I was working closely with Steve on a new project. I'm always smartly dressed at work, but I added a few subtle touches – a slightly lower-cut top, shorter skirts, expensive perfume, retouching my make-up every hour, wearing my hair long instead of tied back. I'd planned to get to work early so we'd be alone in the office together, but I could never quite manage to get out of bed. So I opted for staying late. The trouble was, several people worked late in our office. Getting Steve on his own was going to be tricky. Monday passed, then Tuesday and Wednesday. I started to panic. My interview was on Monday. It had to be soon.

My chance came on the Thursday night. Steve had asked me to put together a summary of our project so far. I'd finished it by mid-afternoon, but I stayed at my computer, poring over it, until Steve and I were the only ones left in our department. Even though I wanted sex with him purely for that promotion, there was definitely some excitement there. The more I looked at him, the hornier I felt. The whole idea turned me on, and I felt myself getting wet at my desk. Each time I looked at Steve, knowing he was blissfully unaware of what I planned to do, I got a real sexual buzz.

Our office is a massive, open-plan space. I could see a couple of people in other departments working away right over the other side, but they were well out of earshot. It was now or never. So I sidled over to Steve's desk, carrying the report, and said, 'D'you fancy going through it in the pub?' I expected Steve to react with a rabbit-caught-in-headlights look, then say yes. But he didn't. He gave me an undeniably sexy look, and said, 'There's some wine in the boardroom. Why don't we go through it in there?'

I followed him upstairs, massively turned on. The boardroom was the only place with no interior windows – just a row overlooking the river – and a lockable door. Steve had a key. Was this heading where I thought it was? It couldn't be. I told myself I was imagining things. I'd never dreamed of using the boardroom. But the way Steve had taken the lead made me even more horny. Neither of us said a word until we got there. He closed the door behind us and locked it, leaving the key in the lock, and saying, 'We don't want the cleaners coming in, do we?' I couldn't believe how easy this was going to be.

Steve poured us a glass of wine while I looked out over the river. He'd created the chance, now all I had to do was go for it. I felt safe. No one could get in. I closed the blinds, gave him a sexy grin and said, 'No one knows we're up here, do they? We could do anything . . .' Then I ran my fingers up the inside of his thigh, over his erection and up his chest. Steve moaned as I touched him and I knew then I was in business.

We kissed each other hard and from there it was fast and very furious. I slid my hand inside his trousers to masturbate him while Steve licked and stroked my breasts. He guided my head down and I sensed he wanted oral sex, so I worked my way down his chest, knelt on the floor, unzipped his trousers and sucked him.

I hope the boardroom is soundproof, because Steve was very, very loud and vocal, talking dirty all the time. He came quickly. I was so close to orgasm that I stood up and kissed him, pulled my knickers aside and masturbated myself. He thrust his fingers inside me, hard, and I came seconds later.

Steve pulled his trousers up quickly, while I did up my blouse. I hadn't even taken off my knickers. I was amazed how turned on I'd been and how easily I'd reached orgasm – what had started out as a ploy to land a job had ended up with great sex. Steve was very businesslike straight away. He said, 'We'd better keep this to ourselves – you don't want anyone thinking you got the job because you give great head!' I grinned. That was fine by me. I went home and masturbated over it.

Next day in the office, Steve was totally normal – no occasional wink, no grins. It was as if it hadn't happened. I felt a bit miffed. I'd given him the blow-job of his life and come in his arms. I hadn't expected to feel put out, but I did. I know I'd started out cold and calculating, but sex isn't like that. Just an acknowledgement of what we'd done would have been fine. But there was nothing, not a flicker. I told myself I'd guaranteed myself the job, so it didn't matter.

My board interview was on the Monday. I was very nervous, but imagining Steve standing by the window with his trousers around his ankles quickly relaxed me. After all, the job was mine. Three days later, the MD called me up to the boardroom. I bounced in, dreaming about what I'd do with the money, grinning to myself at the spot where I'd given him oral sex. Then came the bombshell. 'You're a great asset to the company, Sally.' 'We don't want to lose you, Sally.' 'We hope you'll apply again next time a senior role becomes vacant, Sally.'

They'd given the job to Married Miranda. Obviously a degree from Cambridge and looking like a horse were better qualifications than being damn good at your job and giving great head, I told myself bitterly. When I got back to the office, I was so furious – with myself, as much as anyone – that I couldn't even look at Steve. He came over, totally businesslike, and said he was sorry I hadn't been successful this time. I didn't even look up at him, and I was so demotivated that I was out of the door at 5.30 p.m. on the dot.

What hurt the most was my pride. I'd tried to use someone and ended up getting hurt myself. It was my own fault. But the final blow came a week later, when I was having a drink after work with the girls from the office. Jo, the other girl who'd applied, was there. We ended up very drunk and at a table on our own. She confided that Steve had taken her up to the boardroom a few times 'to run through some interview techniques' and she'd ended up giving him three blow-jobs.

That was when I realised just how stupid I'd been. How many times had he taken girls up there? No one seemed to know what he was doing. Luckily, I was still fairly sober, so I didn't admit to Jo I'd given him oral sex too. Two of Jo's blow-jobs were before mine, but one was the night after. I couldn't believe it. Steve didn't come across as a user, but that's what he was. Mind you, so were we. Talk about exploiting a gap in the market. Steve wanted oral sex – he obviously didn't get it at home – and we wanted promotion. He created the opportunity, and we were stupid enough to go for it. The irony is that I'd bet my life Married Miranda didn't offer her sexual services, and she landed the extra £6,000 p.a.

I stayed in the job for a few weeks, but I couldn't stand working with Steve after that. Every time I looked at him, I hated what I'd done. I've often wondered just how many girls have had sex with him but are too embarrassed to admit it . . .

Sally, 28

She confesses (boy–girl)

I used his boss to get revenge

When Layla decided to get back at her boyfriend for his cruel jibes, she knew just how to do it . . .

It started with a row. Progressed from who last put the rubbish out to full-blown insults. Steve called me 'hopeless'. I wanted to hit back, hard. So I told him his boss, Mike, didn't think so, as he'd been flirting with me all night. It wasn't true, of course. But Mike was a well-known womaniser. Then he uttered the words which changed my life, 'Oh yeah? Mike would never go to bed with you.'

Typically, I'd have yelled, 'We'll see about that', and flounced off. I didn't. This was one argument too many. Steve had eaten away at my confidence with comments like that. There's nothing like anger to make you pull yourself together. How dare he say I wasn't sexy enough to land Mike? That did it. I wanted revenge. I made a silent promise to have sex with his boss, just to spite him.

But it wasn't that simple. For a start, we all worked at the same law firm. Mike was a senior partner, Steve a junior partner and I'm a PA. Practically every woman in the building wanted Mike. He was gorgeous – tall, short dark hair, expensive suit, witty – but he knew it. Married, too, with children. Each time someone flirted with him, I watched his reaction. To act sweet and innocent was my best bet. Everyone else threw themselves at him. I had to be a challenge. The idea of secretly seducing Mike, while he thought he was seducing me, was such a turn-on.

I lost a stone and a half, bought sexier outfits, had a sexy short haircut and felt great about myself. Other men noticed, and that made me feel even better. Mike started to flirt. I played the innocent, inexperienced girlie. Mike was enchanted. Knowing Steve could walk past at any minute added to the thrill – and I bet it turned Mike on, too.

Mike was relentless. He even stopped flirting with other girls. Even my colleagues noticed Mike was 'less of a lad', though they didn't know why. When Steve was out of the office, Mike asked me to lunch. I felt so powerful, so in control, so clever. We started meeting for drinks in the evenings. I told Steve I was going to the gym. The strangest thing was that my relationship with Steve was much better. He'd noticed the change in me and treated me with a lot more respect. He realised his insults didn't work any more. But I still wanted my revenge, and I wanted Mike. The game was addictive and I couldn't stop.

We went to a country pub. The sexual chemistry was explosive. I'd played the game so well that he was desperate. His car was parked at the end of a deserted lane. Halfway down, he kissed me. We'd kissed before, but this was passion like I've never felt. Mike was a master of seduction. He teased me with his fingers, brushing them on my clitoris through my skirt. I protested weakly, saying 'no' or 'we shouldn't'. Mike took my hand and led me under a tree. We kissed again and lay down in the ferns underneath it.

The sex was amazing, far better than I'd dreamed. He was gentle but knew exactly what to do. It was a spring night, but I didn't notice the cold. Once we were on the grass, I gave up my 'sweet and innocent' role, pulled down his trousers and we gave each other oral sex. I couldn't stop myself reaching orgasm, and we came together. But we didn't stop. We kissed until Mike was hard again and had sex twice more. Both of us were pretty forceful. We had sex in every position and made a lot of noise. He'd parked up the lane on purpose, I was sure of it. Maybe it was his regular spot.

I thought Mike would be dismissive, now he'd got what he wanted. But he went all sentimental, talking about the clouds and the sky. It freaked me out. I realised he was hoping to see me again. That wasn't what I wanted at all. He was married with kids, for God's sake. I felt very guilty for all kinds of reasons – Steve, Mike's wife, the fact I'd enjoyed the sex so much. I'd set out for revenge and I'd got it, but my guilt was the price to pay.

Mike was upset when I turned him down. He said I was the only woman he'd ever wanted to see again – apart from his wife. That, I pointed out, was the problem. I didn't admit I'd played a game, so he'd never seen the real me – except when we had sex.

The irony is that Steve and I are still together – and though it's a risky thing to admit, sex with Mike has improved our relationship. I feel so much better about myself. Mike's back to his womanising ways and I do feel jealous when I see him with a girl and think what a treat she's in for.

Layla, 28

He confesses (boy-girl)

I slept with my boss at the office party

Simon didn't even fancy his boss, Anna, but the Christmas party made him see her in a whole new light . . .

Look, I'm going to be blunt about it. My boss, Anna, wasn't the type of woman you look at twice. Great laugh, though. One of the lads. Bit overweight, short dark hair, more Carlsberg than Chardonnay. Just goes to show – you don't know someone till you've had sex with them. Last Christmas Anna and I had the best sex of my life – on her desk.

It was the company's Christmas party. Make that boring-as-hell dinner- dance. Some prat with nothing better to do had drawn up a seating plan. My mate Joe ended up on a raucous table with the blonde from overseas sales. I got some uptight Hooray Henry blokes from finance, a couple of giggly sixteen-year-old typists, and Anna. Thank God there was free booze all night. Joe gave me the thumbs-up every few minutes to really rub it in.

Anna started off her usual loud, bubbly self. By the time they dished up the chicken, the blokes had bored Anna – and me – into silence. So we hit the free booze and talked to each other.

I know what you're thinking. After ten pints of lager, she looked like Claudia Schiffer. Maybe she would have done, but it wasn't like that. I was drunk, but not that drunk.

It started when they brought the ice-cream. Two scoops in a nasty stainless-steel cup. The company had really pushed the boat out. Hardly Häagen-Dazs. But it got us talking about the adverts. And flirting. I noticed how cute she was. Pretty, too. She took off her jacket. At work, I never noticed her clothes. Now I couldn't stop staring. She had on a low-cut black dress. Her breasts were incredible. I went hard just looking at them. I bet her £10 she couldn't eat the ice-cream sexily, without laughing. She did it. I went even harder.

Everything about Anna looked sexier. It wasn't just her clothes and make-up. I was looking at her differently, too. At work, she ran a team of ten sales lads. We respected her. Liked her, even. She was 'one of us'. But no one fancied her – not that I knew about, anyway. Now I wanted her badly. I wanted to touch her breasts, to feel her orgasm – and I didn't know what the hell to do about it.

Women reckon blokes have sex first, think later. Not always. That night, I had a thousand questions. I couldn't answer any of them. Was this a one-night stand? How would we ever work together again? Would I lose my job? Would the guys find out and rip me to shreds? She looked sexy now, but how would I feel on Monday morning?

Maybe you're partly right. I had lots of questions, no answers, but we had some fantastic sex anyway – and I found out the answers later.

We danced. The music slowed. I put my arms round her and her breasts pressed into me. My penis went rock hard against her stomach. I was embarrassed but she looked up at me, smiling. Then she pushed herself against it. I groaned. She said, 'Come on, let's go.'

I didn't know where we were heading. She led me out of the hotel and across the road to our office block. She told the security guard we needed to 'check some details' in the office. He didn't bat an eyelid. I wouldn't have, either. Anna was the last person you'd expect to take her employee up to the sixth floor for sex.

We started in the lift. There was no holding back. Our hands and mouths were everywhere. I sucked and licked her incredible breasts. She undid my trousers and masturbated me fast. Just the right amount of pressure . . .

The doors opened. Anna pulled me out of the lift. She took a swipe card out of her bag to unlock her office, and locked the door behind us. It was dark, but not too dark to see.

Sex was totally explosive. She laid backwards on the desk, on top of files, notes, everything. I pulled her dress off and gave her oral sex, fondling her breasts at the same time. She was soaking wet. I didn't think she'd orgasm so quickly, but she came with a massive shudder and a scream. I pulled her to the edge of the desk and entered her standing up. It was fast, furious, and I was dripping with sweat. When I came, I really let go.

I laid down on top of her, resting my head on a thick sales report. There was a horrible silence. Anna cracked some joke about me getting a promotion, which broke the ice. Then we put what was left of our clothes back on – I'd ripped her bra – and she called us both a cab.

Monday morning was tough. I got in early, but Anna was already at her desk. The desk. I'd spent all weekend wondering how I'd feel, what I should do. Just looking at it made me want to do it all again. Anna had her usual work clothes on, but now I knew what was underneath them. She turned me on without even trying. I couldn't go back to looking at her the way I'd done before.

I asked her out. It was a risk. I didn't even know if she was single. A year on, we're still dating. Sex is still fantastic. Working together was a no-go, so I've transferred to overseas sales – with the blonde I'd always lusted after. I still think she's sexy, but she's not a patch on Anna. The guys can't see why I'm crazy about her. If they go past Anna's office during this year's Christmas party, they might see why. We've got an anniversary to celebrate . . .

Simon, 27

6

Strangers in the Night – or Day

Any time, anywhere. That's the name of the game for this sexy selection. Forget dating, forget breakfast – when these raunchy readers see someone they fancy, they don't want names and phone numbers, they want sex and they want it NOW – in the ladies' loo, on a bus, at a rock concert, in a Jacuzzi . . .

Sex with strangers is risky, and they know it, but for them it's proved the ultimate sexual thrill. Some reveal just how addictive living for the moment can be, and if they're in the mood for a quick one-night (or day) stand, there's always the small ads or the Internet. Just don't – as one red-faced reader reminds us – try videotaping it . . .

She confesses (boy–girl)

I had sex in a Jacuzzi – with a total stranger

When Gina visited her health club, she thought a workout was just what she needed. Then she found what she was really looking for . . .

The moment I walked into the new health club I knew it was right for me. The gym wasn't crammed with guys in tight T-shirts ready to make a move on anyone in Lycra. Nor did the bar feel like an up-market singles club. Just smart, professional people working out or relaxing. So I joined. I wanted to tone up and de-stress – and I fulfilled my ultimate sexual fantasy into the bargain!

It was a bank holiday weekend. My boyfriend was away and even the club was pretty quiet. We'd been through a bad patch and I was so tense with him that reaching orgasm was impossible. Working out at the club took my mind off it. After the gym, I went for a lie in the Jacuzzi. There were a few people in it, but it seats ten comfortably, so I slid into a free seat.

I saw him get in. He was tall, toned and dark-haired. Stunning, in fact. Late twenties, dressed in surfing shorts. We didn't make eye contact. I closed my eyes and rested my head over the edge of the Jacuzzi as he slid into a seat facing me. The water was very hot and the bubbles so fierce that I rested my hands on the edge of my seat to steady myself.

A couple of people got out. I sensed him moving into the seat next to me. As he sat down, our hands accidentally touched. That often happened in the Jacuzzi. But this time, I didn't move my hand away. Neither did he.

I waited for him to move. He didn't. I got the feeling he was waiting for me to move mine. I didn't. Just sensing his fingers on mine turned me on. I couldn't move them away. Sex with a stranger, pure raw sex, was my ultimate desire, my fantasy. Being forced to keep quiet and still when I felt like screaming with pleasure was another fantasy. I kept my eyes closed and my hands on the seat, willing him to touch me. Then I felt his hand slide up my arm. For a second, my hopes sank. Was he just moving his arm away? He slid his arm behind me. I stayed still. Slowly, I felt his fingers on my back, stroking me. Now I knew it was real. I couldn't believe it. Both fantasies were coming true at once.

I half-opened my eyes. Two other people were still in the Jacuzzi. Even if things didn't go any further, it was the biggest turn-on I'd ever experienced. He carried on stroking my back, slipping his fingers into the top crease of my bottom.

Then everyone else got out. I couldn't stop now. My clitoris was throbbing. I wanted to masturbate, but part of the fantasy was keeping still, so I left my hands on the seat and eased open my legs. He sensed what I needed, slid his fingers inside my swimming costume and stroked my clitoris. I knew I was going to come quickly. People were sitting beside the Jacuzzi on sun-loungers, so I had to keep still and quiet. When I came, I wanted to scream. I don't know how I stopped myself. I hope the raging bubbles hid my shudders of delight. It was the best orgasm I've ever had.

All this time, my hands were still gripping the seat. I hadn't touched him, or looked at him. He took my hand and led me out of the Jacuzzi, to one of the empty changing cubicles at the far end of the club. That's when I got my first real look at him. We smiled at each other, and I was relieved to see he was as good-looking as I thought. Then we had fast, furious, silent sex, standing up. I didn't come again, but I loved the feeling of him inside me.

Afterwards, part of me wanted him – or me – to leave without a word. That way my fantasy would be preserved. He'd stay faceless, nameless. But in reality there was no way we could do that. I didn't want him to think I made a habit out of this, and I guess he didn't want me to think he was a total bastard. His first words were, 'Do you fancy a swim?' Even his voice was sexy. Still in shock, I nodded. So we did a few lengths in the pool. My head was spinning. I got out and sat on a sun-lounger. He sat beside me and chatted, asking how often I visited the club, whether I liked it . . . Neither of us mentioned what we'd just done. It was surreal. But I sensed this was a first for him, too. When we accidentally touched hands, it had triggered a hidden sexual desire in both of us.

I enjoyed chatting to him, but I didn't want to see him again. It was fantastic, but I had a boyfriend and was already feeling the odd pang of guilt. When he said he'd come to the club as a one-off, as he was working in the area for a couple of days, I was relieved. That meant I wouldn't bump into him again.

He gave me his number and offered me a lift home. I went into the changing rooms and said I'd see him in the car park. That's when it hit me. I had just had rampant sex with a total stranger. Getting into a car with him was a crazy idea. So I left the club by the front entrance and went home.

I haven't seen him since, but I don't regret what I did. It was the best orgasm I've ever had, and I've fantasised about it endlessly. I'd definitely do it again if the moment was right. I was on such a high that sex with my boyfriend was spiced up too!

Gina, 26

He confesses (boy–girl)

From rush-hour hell to the ride of my life

When Iain broke down on his way to work, he didn't expect to end his journey in a hotel room with a sexy stranger . . .

Monday morning rush hour. Had to be in the bloody rush hour. My car packed up in a traffic jam. I had a meeting with clients in central London. Was I in the AA? Was I hell. It wasn't just the car overheating. I'd had a gutful. Every driver crawling past gave me a 'you unlucky bastard' look. Or a smirk. Two hours later, I was the one smirking. They didn't know how lucky I was going to get.

I needed a lift to the nearest station. I figured I'd sort out the bloody car later. So I stuck out my thumb and hoped a lorry driver would stop. She pulled up alongside me, opened her window and asked if I was OK.

Maybe it was the steam coming out of the bonnet that convinced her. Maybe I just don't look like an axe murderer. Maybe there was so much traffic that she felt safe. Whatever, she offered me a lift into town.

We chatted. She worked in PR. No wedding ring. I tried not to stare at her, but she was gorgeous. A classic blonde. Long straight hair, big eyes, perfect breasts under the tight T-shirt. Long, long legs in white jeans. Very toned. I couldn't see her bum but I knew it would be tight, just how I like it. Every single guy stores up images like that, no matter what they say. It's healthy. Trust me.

The traffic wasn't moving. We both phoned ahead to say we'd be late. That's when she started flirting. Up till then, I'd played it straight. I didn't want her to think I was some sex-mad hitchhiker. Now I knew she was interested. I couldn't believe my luck. I flirted back and hoped I'd get her phone number. But I didn't think we'd have sex half an hour later.

We reached a junction. She pulled off and said we'd try the 'back roads'. The sexual chemistry was intense, fever pitch. We both stared at the motel up ahead. I wanted to say, 'Let's book a room,' but I didn't have the guts. I guess I was afraid of scaring her off. I shouldn't have worried. She drove into the car park, turned off the engine and said, 'Are you up for it?' I kissed her. Our hands were all over each other. We masturbated each other in the car and almost had sex in it. She stopped and said, 'Let's go to bed.'

We checked in as Mr and Mrs Smith and talked in a loud voice about 'driving all night' and 'needing some sleep'. I don't know why we bothered. Looking back, at 10 a.m. it was so obvious we were there for sex. They asked if we wanted the special 'day rate'. Check out by 3 p.m. Sounded good to me. I paid. It seemed fair. After all, she'd given me a lift.

There was no awkward pause, no 'what do we do now?' We

started the moment she shut the bedroom door. It was the best sex of my life. She undressed me as we kissed and gave me oral sex on the bed until I was on the verge of orgasm. I didn't think I could hold back, but I did. Then she kissed me all over, slowly, until I'd calmed down enough for her to climb on top. She took me to the edge of orgasm, over and over again. It felt like my balls were going to explode. This was Heaven.

I slid down the bed and gave her oral sex. When she came, it was incredible. I felt every muscle in her body shaking. She totally let go. Then she slid back down onto my penis. I was so ready to come. It was the loudest, most intense orgasm I've ever had in my life.

Afterwards, neither of us could believe we'd done it. But the atmosphere was fine. She had a shower while I made a coffee in the room. Her mobile rang. I knew by her face it was the boyfriend. She told him she was 'still stuck in traffic' and looked embarrassed. I grinned and said, 'Don't worry, I'm in a relationship too.' I wasn't. I wanted to save face. She said, 'I'm glad I'm not the only one who's been naughty.'

I said I'd ring for a cab to the nearest station. She looked relieved. The adrenaline had stopped pumping, it was 11.30 a.m. on a Monday morning and I was back in the real world. If she'd been single, I would have loved to see her again. But I knew from that phone call there was no chance. It had happened, it was amazing, now I needed to get to work and move on.

She left first. I couldn't resist asking why she'd done it. She said simply, 'I really fancied you.' A year on, I still get a kick out of that.

Iain, 29

She confesses (boy–girl)

I did get my satisfaction

Maria knew she'd have a good time at the Rolling Stones concert, but she didn't realise it would involve sex with two different men in less than two hours . . .

I couldn't say no. An all-expenses-paid trip to London to see the Rolling Stones was just what I needed. I'd spent far too long moping around my flat, waiting for Nick to call. Nick was my ex. He was one of those guys you want to hate but can't. So when his best friend, Phil, invited me to the concert, I said yes. Sex wasn't on my agenda. Sure, I guessed it was on his, but I could handle that. I was right. I did handle it – by having sex with both Phil and a total stranger.

We arrived at the Holiday Inn at lunchtime. Phil sorted out our reservation and led the way to our rooms. Make that room, complete with double bed. Phil mumbled something about 'saving money with one room'. I made it clear he was to sleep on the sofa.

The pub next to the stadium was packed with people on their way to the concert. Some were spilling out onto the pavement, singing and laughing. '19th Nervous Breakdown' blared out into the heat. The atmosphere was electric. We took our drinks outside and got chatting to a group of lads from Wales. That's when I saw Jon. A younger George Clooney. Come-to-bed eyes, a quiet voice and a sexy smile that made me want to give him a blow-job right there on the pavement.

God, I sound like an easy lay. I'm not. I've never done anything like it, before or since. The sun, the atmosphere, the Pimms, being dumped by Nick – and the fact Jon was the horniest guy I'd seen for years – had a strange effect on me. He whispered, 'Take your sunglasses off – I want to see your eyes.'

Sounds corny? I agree. But that afternoon, on that pavement, it made me hotter than ever. I knew that sex with him would be incredible. With some guys, you just know.

Everyone left the pub together. I stuck close to Jon, but when we got inside the stadium, he headed for the front. Phil was strictly a 'let's stay near the back by the emergency exit or we might get crushed' kind of guy. Sex with Phil was now definitely out of the question – I knew exactly what that would be like, too. Or so I thought. . .

Dutifully, I stayed with Phil. But the beat was amazing, I couldn't stop thinking about Jon and I didn't want him to get away. So I yelled to Phil, 'I'm going up the front', and disappeared into the crowds.

There were literally thousands of people dancing. I pushed my way to the edge, hoping to see Jon somewhere, when I felt a hand on my shoulder. I still don't know if he'd been watching me, waiting for me to get away from Phil. We hugged and I felt his erection pressing against me through his jeans. I'd never wanted sex with a stranger before, but I was so horny that I felt like exploding.

Jon grabbed my hand and we pushed our way out of the stadium. Neither of us said a word. I didn't even have my ticket, so I knew I couldn't get back into the stadium, but I didn't care. We found a deserted spot round the back of the stadium and kissed. Knowing we could get caught at any moment just added to the thrill.

I was wearing a mini-dress. Jon kissed me all the way down the front of it, then put his head under my skirt, pulled down my knickers and gave me oral sex. My clitoris was so swollen and horny that I was near to orgasm before he even licked me. At first, I kept a lookout – and got a kick out of seeing his head under my dress – but when he pushed his fingers inside me, I had to close my eyes and go with it. I came very loudly.

Jon stood up and we both tugged down his jeans. Even

though I'd reached orgasm, I wanted to feel him inside me. We had fast, hard sex against the wall, talking dirty. The bricks scraped against my bottom, but the sex was far too good to stop. Neither of us noticed that the music had stopped. As Jon came, I heard the sound of thousands of fans bursting out of the stadium. He pulled up his jeans, I pulled up my knickers and Jon said, 'Can I have your phone number?' We swapped numbers but I knew neither of us would ever call. I didn't regret it, because I knew I'd never have sex like it again.

That's when I realised I had no room key and no idea where the hotel was. Everyone wanted a taxi, and I had to wait more than an hour. Then the driver said, 'Which Holiday Inn?' I had no idea there were more than one.

We eventually found the right hotel. Phil had left me a key at reception, so I crept in quietly. He was asleep in bed. There was no way I was sleeping on the sofa, so I got in beside him. The bed was really warm. I was still horny. I thought about masturbating, but when Phil reached over and stroked my nipples, I let him. The sex was gentle and caring, with masturbation and then full sex – in the missionary position – which was just what I felt like after my session with Jon.

Phil and I ended up dating for a few weeks. Sex between us was OK, but it was never explosive, and was never going to be. He only mentioned the concert once, saying, 'I don't know what happened that night and I don't want to know.' I'm sure he really knew.

Maria, 26

She confesses (boy–girl)

My pre-wedding fling saved my marriage

An on-line chat with a stranger was just what Hannah needed to cure her relationship doubts . . .

Married? Off the market? Sex with one man for the rest of my life? I couldn't go through with it . . . could I? My sister called it 'pre-wedding nerves'. That was an understatement. More like 'pre-wedding paranoia'. But I found the ultimate cure – 24 hours of sex with a guy I met on the Internet. After that, I was cool about walking down the aisle.

I've been married for a year now, and my husband Pete has no idea what I got up to. I really do love him, and I'm so glad I got away with it. The bloody wedding preparations were half the problem. We were so wrapped up in caterers and florists – let alone my dress – that we pretty much neglected each other. Our sex life was the worst hit. After three years together, we knew exactly how to turn each other on, and had great sex, most nights. Suddenly he was working all hours to pay for the wedding, and we were both tired, stressed and bickering. Sex became a complete no-no.

Things got so bad that I wanted to call it off. My friends and my sister tried to reassure me. There were two months to go until the wedding. With Pete at work most nights, I looked for company on the Internet. I couldn't believe how many people in chat rooms were obviously looking for cybersex. Many of the messages started out flirty and went downhill from there. I was frustrated, bored and couldn't help joining in. Soon I was having cybersex with different guys most nights, masturbating myself to orgasm at my computer in the living room as the messages got steamier. Some of the guys even emailed me their phone numbers and I had phone sex with them too.

I didn't feel guilty – after all, I wasn't technically being unfaithful. I had no idea who these guys were, where they came from or what they looked like. Sometimes they suggested meeting up, but I was totally honest with them – I said I was getting married and was just out for some no-strings cybersex or phone sex. They were fine about that. For me, it was less risky than picking someone up in a bar – and it was addictive.

One guy, Dan, was different. We didn't start out flirting in the chat room, we just talked. Something clicked and soon we were on the phone to each other for over an hour every day. He was a single, sweet and funny IT worker. Our relationship became quite intense. I confided in him about my pre-wedding nerves and he was a really good listener. One evening, I joked that I hadn't had sex for three months. The talk turned dirty and, after a very raunchy conversation, we began having phone sex. When he suggested meeting up, I knew I wanted to. The way I was feeling, I couldn't go through with the wedding. Perhaps having sex with him would tell me if marrying Pete was the right thing to do.

He lived in London, I was in Birmingham. So I told Pete I was away overnight on a course, booked a hotel halfway and confided in a friend, so someone knew where I was. I hadn't had proper sex for weeks, and I was desperate. There was no point meeting in a restaurant, pretending that nothing would happen – we were going to sleep with each other. I needed to.

I wanted to get there first, freshen up, and be sitting on the bed, reading, looking sexy, when he arrived. But my train was delayed. Talk about frayed nerves – I was jumpy, excited and horny, all at once. I phoned his mobile to say I'd be late and he offered to pick me up from the station. When I got there, I couldn't see anyone, so I called his mobile again. We were still talking on the phone when he pulled up beside me.

I'll be honest – Dan wasn't a male model. But he had a fabulous smile, a larger-than-life personality and I fancied him like crazy. I felt I knew him so well that it didn't really matter what he looked like. We'd already had some great phone sex, now I wanted the real thing. We carried on talking to each other on the mobiles as I got in the car. That really broke the ice. I grinned and said, 'Shall I turn the phone off now?' He smiled, leaned across and kissed me. There was real warmth in his kiss, and I felt sure I'd done the right thing. My only fear was that I'd fall in love with him and have to call off the wedding . . .

I checked in to the hotel quickly while he parked the car, so I got to the room first. It was only 1 p.m., so we were both sober, but I shouldn't have worried. He came in, dropped his bags, sat down on the bed and kissed me. The sex wasn't frenzied – it was slow and sensual. We took off each other's clothes slowly, gently, and he masturbated me to orgasm. I came easily. Then he climbed on top and came quickly. We turned on the TV, ate crisps, drank Coke and lay naked on the bed, laughing and chatting, totally relaxed in each other's company.

By morning, we'd had sex six times. I did enjoy it, but as time went on, I found it harder and harder to reach orgasm. I'd called Pete several times on my mobile, too, pretending I was on the course – and Dan had phoned his wife. I started feeling guilty and ready to go home.

Luckily I was due at work the next morning, so Dan knew I'd be leaving very early. I said I'd had a great time, and hoped we'd stay in touch, making it clear that meeting up was a one-off. He looked upset, but accepted it and gave me a gentle kiss goodbye. He didn't contact me again.

When I saw Pete that evening, I knew more than ever I wanted to marry him. And two weeks later, the wedding went ahead. We'd agreed we wouldn't have sex on our wedding night – we'd both had so much pressure on us, it was a recipe for disaster. But the next morning, I woke up to Pete gently kissing my breasts, then giving me wonderful oral sex. He gave me the most amazing orgasm. In a way, I regret my fling, but I know if I hadn't gone ahead with it, I wouldn't have married Pete. And that would have meant a lifetime of missing out on sexy Sundays.

Hannah, 27

She confesses (boy–girl)

I secretly filmed my one-night stand

Joanna's fantasy was to videotape her sex session with a handsome stranger. Then the tape disappeared . . .

Porn films turned me on. Still do. But my ultimate fantasy was to watch myself having sex. Real, hot, frenzied sex. On videotape. Just for my personal use, you understand. I could relive every stroke, every lick, whenever I felt like it. So I set up a secret video camera, picked up a guy in a club and had the wildest sex of my life. Then the tape disappeared . . .

It was totally out of character. Honest. Five long-term relationships and not a single one-night stand, until that night. I'm sure my ex-boyfriends would have been up for starring in our own porn film. But sex with them was big on emotion, short on passion. Too caring. Not the raw, wild sex I had in mind for my film. And what would we do with the tape if we split up? No, I wanted something hot. Something I could keep. Something I was emotionally detached from.

Then I saw an episode of Ricki Lake's chat show. Two American guys admitted secretly taping their one-night stands. They even compared techniques afterwards. I was horrified. Turned on, too. The idea got in my head and wouldn't go away. I wanted to make that tape. If men could do it, so could I.

I borrowed the camera from my friend Angie. For my 'niece's sports day', of course. A few glasses of wine later, I confessed. Angie thought it was hilarious. She didn't think I'd do it. Nor did I. But she showed me how to use the camera anyway.

My wardrobe had to be the best place. Right at the foot of my bed. I hid the camera among the stuffed animals on top of it. But I couldn't be sure if the bed was even in the picture, so I climbed on top of the wardrobe and peered through the viewfinder. It took a lot of fiddling to get it right. I had to laugh at myself, perched up on the wardrobe, but I was excited. Horny, too. Now all I needed was a man.

Picking up Joe was easy. We were on a girls' night out. I'd seen him in the club before, eyeing me up, but this time I smiled back. Nerves and excitement made me flirt like crazy, and just thinking about the video made me wet. I wanted him in it. He came in for coffee. I'd had a lot to drink but I knew exactly what I was doing. I slipped into the bedroom and pushed 'play'. Now all I had to do was get him in there and keep the bedside light on.

We started on the sofa, kissing and touching. I wanted this on my film, so I breathed, 'Let's go into the bedroom.' He undressed me right in front of the camera. I wanted to crouch down and give him oral sex, but I wasn't sure if I'd be on film. So I pushed him onto the bed, laid across his chest and licked his penis, facing the camera. Knowing I could relive it all on film brought me close to orgasm before he'd even touched me.

I didn't forget about the camera for a second. We had sex in every position, and I kept him on the bed, always in view of the camera. Joe came loudly three times. The sex was amazing, and I almost came several times. I didn't want to orgasm too soon, though, so I stopped myself. It was weird – I actually went past the point of orgasm. By the time we collapsed with exhaustion, I still hadn't come, but I wasn't worried. I knew I could masturbate over it again in the morning.

When I woke up, Joe was still there. I went through to the

kitchen and made us coffee and toast, hoping that he'd eat and leave. He did. Excited, I climbed up and pushed 'eject'. The tape wasn't there.

I panicked. What could have happened to it? I told myself I'd forgotten to put the tape in. But the empty wrapper was on top of the wardrobe. I had to accept it – Joe had taken the tape.

That week was the longest of my life. I even confessed to Angie. I didn't even dare go to the pub, in case he'd made copies. Our town is small enough for lads to recognise you if you've just starred in a home movie. I wished I'd never made the tape. No fantasy was worth the hell I went through. Worst of all, I felt I deserved it.

Days later, Joe turned up at my flat. I wasn't angry – I was relieved. At last I could find out the truth. I wanted to blurt out, 'What have you done with the tape?' but I still didn't know for sure that he'd taken it. We chatted politely for a few minutes, then Joe asked if I was wondering about the tape.

I thought I'd be furious, but I couldn't stop apologising. Joe grinned. He said he'd seen the little flashing red light on the front of the camera among my soft toys, and guessed I was taping him. That's why he stayed the night. While I made breakfast, he took out the tape.

I was shaking as I asked what he'd done with it. He told me to look down the back of my bed. We went upstairs, and I reached down behind the headboard. The tape was there. It had been there all week. He'd done it to teach me a lesson. To be honest, I deserved it. I've never been so relieved. I was lucky Joe was such a decent guy, and we have stayed friends.

Joe and I agreed to destroy the tape, so we smashed it together. I didn't want to watch it, not even secretly. After what I went through, I couldn't get horny watching myself having sex if I tried.

Joanna, 22

He confesses (boy–girl)

My health club heaven

Richard used to fantasise about the sexy woman he saw at the gym. Little did he know she was planning to get physical with him . . .

Fit, toned girls send me into a sexual seventh heaven. But this girl – I'll call her Sam, though I still don't know her name – was a cut above the rest. Sam was one of those girls you idolise from afar. I'd seen her on the cross-trainer and her workout put mine to shame. Not surprising, as her boyfriend was one of the gym instructors. I privately nicknamed him 'Arnie'. Then he was off sick one afternoon, and Sam and I had the workout of our lives.

Sam used the gym every afternoon, always when Arnie was on duty. She still does. It's a posh health club, all halogen spotlights and stainless steel. I'd been a member for a year and always worked out on my days off. I'm a doctor – senior house officer in a hospital A&E. I was careful not to stare at Sam – Arnie didn't look the tolerant type – but I organised my workout so I was on equipment close to her. She isn't Swedish, but she looks it – tall, with long blonde hair, tied back, and model looks. For all I know, she is a model.

We'd smiled at each other and nodded, like you do in the gym when you see someone regularly. I'd masturbated thinking about her, too. She was a total fantasy figure – perfect looks, but untouchable. When I made love to my girlfriend, sometimes I pretended she was Sam. I always used the gym's unisex sauna and steam room, hoping Sam would come in – but she never did. To be honest, I didn't seriously think I stood a chance of having sex with her. I'm good-looking – so girls tell me – and I'm fit, but Sam was in a different league. Or so I thought.

Talk about fate. The afternoon it happened, I was supposed

to be at work. Then we swapped our rotas around. I'd been out with the lads for a few too many beers the night before, and I'd got a cold, so I didn't plan on going to the gym at all. But by lunchtime, I was bored. My girlfriend was at work, so I popped to the gym for a quick sauna.

It was midsummer, so the gym was pretty quiet. Sam was there, on a running machine. I decided to have a quick workout. There were so many empty machines that I'd look ridiculous taking the one next to her, so I took one behind. I didn't want to sweat out all the beer right next to her, and that gave me a chance to look at her, too. Her body was amazing. She was wearing a Lycra cropped top and leggings that stopped at the knee. I'll try not to go on about her bum, but I couldn't stop staring at it. Anna Kournikova had nothing on her. Even though I was jogging, I felt myself going hard. My training shorts are baggy, but not that baggy. This wasn't the time to get a massive erection, so I stared at MTV until it subsided. I was dehydrated, so I stopped jogging and went to the water dispenser. As I filled my cup, someone was standing behind me. It was Sam.

She smiled and bent down to refill her water bottle. I glanced round the gym. Arnie wasn't in view. I hadn't seen him since I arrived. So I decided to risk it. I said, 'Hi, isn't your boyfriend working today?'

The moment the words came out of my mouth, I realised they sounded like some cheap chat-up line. But she grinned, said, 'No, he's off sick with the flu,' and walked over to the cross-trainer before I could say a word. It sounds crazy, but I was glad about that. I was like a tongue-tied teenager. Saved me blabbing on about flu cases in A&E and totally destroying my chances.

Did she fancy me? I couldn't quite believe it, but there had definitely been a sexual chemistry between us. We didn't make eye contact on the cross-trainers, and I decided it was all in my head. Wishful thinking. Then she moved on to other equipment, and I followed.

The machines are arranged in a huge circle. When it's busy, you're always facing someone directly opposite. Pretty off-putting if there's some huge, unfit whale of a guy across from you. But Sam and I were the only people in there. The instructors were at their station, chatting, taking no notice of either of us. Sam chose the equipment opposite me. I figured it was chance. Then she did it again. We made eye contact. Now I knew she was interested.

The sexual thrill that went through me was something else. Each time she caught my eye, she gave me a sexy smile. I couldn't concentrate on working out at all. She wasn't just interested, she was up for sex. But what could I do? The instructors weren't in earshot, but they could see us.

Sam walked across the gym and took the machine next to me. She whispered, 'What would you say if I suggested our own personal workout?'

I couldn't believe what she'd just said. My mind went into overdrive, computing and re-computing, making sure she meant what I thought she meant. I still couldn't be sure, so I replied, 'I'd say yes.' She said, 'Meet me in the ladies' toilets near the bar in ten minutes,' picked up her water bottle and disappeared into the changing rooms.

To be honest, I was terrified. My dream might be about to come true and what was I doing? Bloody panicking. What if this was a set-up? It sounded too good. What if Arnie was in there? What if another woman was in there? What if she just didn't show up? I was bound to end up looking a total prat. Not good. I went for a shower while I decided what to do. Usually after a workout I masturbated in the shower cubicle, but not today. I was so nervous that I didn't even get an erection at first. But as the warm water ran over me, I calmed down, stopped being so negative and imagined what it would be like if Sam was in there. My penis hardened, but I stopped myself masturbating. There was a real chance she was up for it, and I had to find out for sure.

I had to hand it to her – it was a quiet place to meet. Hardly anyone used the toilets by the bar. Maybe she'd done it before.

By the time I got outside the ladies loo, my heart was thumping. Excitement, nerves – I had the lot. I waited a minute in case anyone came out, then pushed the door open.

My first thought was, 'Thank God there's no one by the basins.' I checked the cubicles and realised she wasn't in there. Was I devastated? Too bloody right. I felt so stupid. Then the door opened behind me and I got ready with my excuses, but I didn't need them. It was Sam. She'd showered – I could smell the expensive soap. Her hair was still slightly wet, and she was wearing a cropped top and jogging pants. She pushed me backwards into the end cubicle and shut the door.

We kissed each other hard. My hands were all over her, feeling her bum, her breasts, her legs, her taut stomach. I couldn't believe I was touching her. My penis went so hard that I had to press it against her. Right then I didn't care if anyone came in and heard us. She undid my jeans and masturbated me so fast and hard that I had to pull her off to stop myself coming.

Sam leaned against the wall and pushed down her jogging pants. I pulled down her knickers and gave her oral sex while squeezing and feeling her bottom. She moaned quietly, but still loud enough for someone to hear. I was still too close to orgasm to masturbate, or to care if anyone heard us. I licked my way up to her breasts and pushed up her top. She wasn't wearing a bra. I took her nipples in my mouth and she said, 'I want you inside me.' I can't tell you what a kick those words gave me. I've masturbated over them so many times since. I knew I'd come quickly, but she sat me down on the loo seat, took off her jogging pants, hung them on the back of the door and straddled me. I rubbed her clitoris with my finger as she moved up and down. I came almost straight away, with a very loud groan. She came a few seconds later.

Afterwards, she straightened her clothes, gave me a kiss and said, 'That was wild. Our secret, right?' Then she left. I was still sitting on the toilet seat, trousers and pants round my ankles.

I didn't move for a couple of minutes. I didn't even care that I was in the ladies, or that anyone who'd come in would have heard us. Or that the bloody club probably had CCTV in the loos. I didn't even feel guilty. I was just totally sexually satisfied and, if I'm honest, in a state of shock. Things like that just don't normally happen to me.

When I recovered, reality hit and I realised that a: I was in the ladies toilets and b: if any staff had come in and heard us, Arnie would find out. I got dressed, making sure I was quiet, slipped out of the loo and went home, not even going back to collect my gym bag.

I didn't go back to the gym for two or three weeks. My gear in the gym bag was in a right state. Call me a coward if you like – I admit it, I was scared. I told all my mates about it, of course, though I'm not sure they believed me. I even got one of them to come with me the next time I went to the gym, just in case Arnie had found out. Sam was there – and Arnie. He nodded as I went in, like he always did. I was sure he didn't know. Sam didn't acknowledge me at first, but when Arnie went up the far end, she smiled and winked. I winked back. My girlfriend still doesn't know, and I do fantasise about Sam sometimes when we have sex. It's deeper with my girlfriend, more loving, but that session with Sam was incredible. I still go to the gym, and they're both still there. Sam and I smile, but nothing more. Arnie has been off a few times, but Sam hasn't suggested a repeat performance. Shame, because I'd be up for it. People say fantasies never live up to your expectations in real life, but sex with Sam was even better.

Richard, 34

She confesses (boy–girl)

I found love in the small ads

Samantha wanted no-strings sex – and she found the perfect man to give it to her . . .

I know what you're thinking: what kind of sad, unattractive girl picks up a man through the small ads? So let's get it straight. I was 24 and worked in advertising. Known in the business as 'a bit of a babe'. So the lads told me, anyway. Now I sound like I'm writing my own lonely-hearts ad. But all the men I ever met wanted commitment. I didn't. Just sex was fine by me. Life was too much fun to get tied down and trapped. Then I saw his ad in a national newspaper – and got exactly what I wanted. For one night only.

I've read the lonely-hearts columns ever since I was a teenager. I love the way people describe themselves, and enjoy trying to work out whether the 'handsome, young company director' – why are they always company directors? – is really some sad, retired postman with a penchant for women under 35. It should be declared a sport in itself. It's always good for a giggle and, if they sound sexy, a fantasy. I'd masturbated over the idea so many times, imagining the thrill of going to meet that 'single male', wondering what he'd look like and finding he was gorgeous, taking him back to my flat and having wild, raw sex with him. No commitment and no breakfast.

Now that the ads sometimes include voice messages too, it's even better. A voice gives away so much. The trouble was, every one I'd dialled for a laugh sounded either seriously old or seriously odd. Until I rang Peter.

I'd had a heavy day at work, so decided what better way to relax than with a take-away pizza (diet tomorrow), a chilled bottle of Frascati and the paper. When I reached the lonely-hearts section, Peter's ad caught my eye straight away. No 'good sense of humour', no 'seeks friendship, maybe more'. Just, 'Do you want to have fun? Commitment-phobic guy, 25, does too. Girls ask me out, so looks must be OK. No strings, no husband-hunters.'

There had to be a catch. Ugly as sin, I bet. Or lying. But I dialled anyway, and listened to his message out of curiosity. He sounded sexy, and well-spoken, too. His name was Peter, and he worked as a software consultant. Hmm. Bound to be a nerd. Big glasses and spots. But there was something about him. . . By the time I'd finished my bottle of Frascati, I'd phoned back and left my mobile number. Said I was commitment-phobic too, but if he fancied a no-strings drink, to give me a call.

Next morning, I hated myself for doing it. Was I crazy? How the hell could I go for a drink with a total stranger? What if he turned into a phone pest, or somehow traced my home address? Sure, it was a quality broadsheet newspaper, but I knew that anyone could advertise in it. I tormented myself until lunchtime, when he rang.

Peter sounded gorgeous. Could he speak to Samantha, please? I knew it was him. He said, 'Hi, I'm Peter. I got your message.' That voice just breathed sex. I blurted out, 'Hi, do you work in London too?' Why the hell did I say that? But it got us chatting. He gave me his surname and office number. Did I want to meet for a drink, Friday night? I wasn't sure, but I agreed anyway. Outside his office at 7 p.m. What the hell. I could always stand him up.

The idea was such a turn-on that I couldn't say no. I masturbated about him that night, fantasising how it would feel when he touched me, had sex with me. Then I told myself to get a life. He was bound to be vile. But maybe, just maybe . . .

I checked out his company on the Internet. Peter was listed as a software developer. So far, so good. Genuine. No photo, though. By Friday afternoon, I'd confided in the entire agency staff, all my friends and a trusted ex-boyfriend, who helpfully suggested I was a lunatic. I went anyway.

The office was very plush, all marble staircase and model-like receptionists. I asked for Peter Smith. He'd be down in a minute. Then a guy appeared at the top of the stairs. Couldn't be him. No way. No computer geek ever looked like Val Kilmer. Only in films. Mid-length blond hair, brushed back, big eyes, and a body to die for. Not a spot in sight. I'm not into suits, but this one was pure style. Expensive and well cut, though I reckoned he'd look good in anything. Preferably nothing. Maybe I could ask him out instead.

I focused my gaze on the top of the stairs, waiting for a Bill Gates lookalike to show. Actually, I felt like darting out of the building. But the gorgeous guy walked up to me and said, 'Samantha? Hi, I'm Peter.' Relief was written all over my face. His too. He fancied me, I knew it. This was going to be a good night.

We went to the bar of a big London hotel. That was my suggestion. I felt safer there, and if this worked, we could take a room. I phoned my flatmate, as I'd promised, to tell her exactly where I was. He didn't look like a weirdo, but you can't be too careful. When I went to the loo, I made sure my drink was empty, and we sat at the bar so I could see the bartender pour the drinks out. God, I sound paranoid. But I'd read about date-rape drugs, and I wasn't taking any risks. I wanted to be fully in control.

The flirting started straight away. Why wait? That's what we were there for and the sexual attraction between us was hot. If I'd met him in a bar, I'd have fancied him anyway. But expecting Bill Gates and getting Val Kilmer was just too good to be true. If the sex didn't happen tonight, then it had to be soon. But I wanted it to be tonight.

Why had he advertised, when he was so good-looking? Because every girl saw him as a 'good catch'. They were buying bridal magazines by the third date and making sure he wanted children. He'd had ten replies to his ad, but I was the only person he'd arranged to meet. Why? Because I sounded just like him. After three drinks, we were swapping fantasies. He dreamed of having sex in a thunderstorm, or on a wild beach, with the waves crashing down. I wanted to be the person he did it with. I told him how I wanted to be made love to on a deserted tropical beach, or in the sea. I didn't confess that my lonely-heart fantasy was coming true, right now. After four drinks, I was so turned on I asked if he'd like to book a room.

Peter said, 'Are you sure?'. I was dead sure. He wouldn't let me pay, so I gave in after a few weak protests. Sorry if I let down the side, girls, but that £100 would go nicely towards my next Karen Millen dress. Then I rang my friend on my mobile and left the room number on her answerphone. I wanted him to know I'd done that, just to be sure. We started kissing in the lift. By the time he'd swiped the door key in the lock fifteen times, I'd got his jacket and tie off.

We didn't even make it to the bed. As we fell through the door and onto the floor, I kicked the door shut and literally ripped the rest of his clothes off. I gave him oral sex, then he went down on me. It was the most frenzied, wildest sex. When he touched my clitoris with his tongue for the first time, it was like an amazing electric shock, right through my body. Every nerve in my body was shaking. We rolled into the bathroom and Peter turned on the power shower. Every time I take a shower, I remember that delicious feeling of hot water running down us as we masturbated each other to orgasm. I still masturbate in showers about it.

Afterwards, we put on the hotel bathrobes, ordered pizza from room service and watched MTV in total bliss. I didn't want to leave, but we'd had a no-strings deal, so I felt I ought to. Peter just said, 'Why waste it? Let's stay the night and have breakfast.' So we did. Joanne, my friend, woke me on the phone at 6 a.m. to check I was OK. Then we made love again.

Peter and I ended up dating for two years. Tentatively, at first, because neither of us wanted to go back on the deal. We'd call each other and go round in circles until one of us cracked and said, 'Shall we meet up?' We'd promised no strings and we were desperately trying to stick to it. After three months, he told me he loved me. I'll never forget how scared he looked, terrified I'd tell him to back off. But I didn't. I told him I loved him too. Sometimes we went to the hotel and pretended to be strangers, then went up to the room and relived our fantasy. Sex between us was always good, but it was never as wild as that first night. I've never been tempted by the small ads since, or even fantasised about them. I don't need to – I've lived it. With Peter, I know I got lucky.

Samantha, 26

She confesses (boy–girl)

I had my fantasy man non-stop for Christmas

Tammy wasn't looking forward to the journey home after seeing her parents at Christmas – until Greg came on board . . .

Forget tall, dark and handsome. He was short, blond and stocky. But he oozed sex appeal. Like Robbie Williams. He wasn't your classic good-looking guy, but he breathed sex from every pore. I knew he'd be good at it. And I spent the next two days finding out just how good. Eight incredible orgasms is the best Christmas present I've ever had.

I'd been visiting my parents. The usual pre-Christmas get-together, then five hours on a coach back through the Scottish

Highlands. It was easier than driving. Duty done, I wanted to get home and start Christmas partying with my friends. Then he got on – and I spent the next 48 hours in sexual heaven.

I'd fantasised about my ideal guy but I didn't think he really existed. Now I was face to face with him. The shoulder-length sandy hair, the dark skin, the athletic body – he was perfect. Just looking at him made me wet. Did I stay cool and give him a sultry look? Did I hell. I was so shocked that I stared at him with my mouth open.

He walked up the coach towards me and caught my eye. My cheeks burned red. He knew I fancied him. But it was far more than that. I had to have him. I couldn't let him get away. I'd never picked up a stranger, never wanted to, but this guy was different. I felt I knew him already. I'd fantasised about him often enough.

He grinned and took the seat in front of me. I wanted to reach through the gap in the seats and touch him. He got out a book. Intellectual, too. Well-travelled, judging by the Qantas label on his bag. Then he turned round and asked me the time.

We didn't stop talking. Greg was 28, Australian and a doctor. He'd spent three months travelling round Britain, and was due to fly out to India in two days' time. Two days. Two whole days. My mind went into overdrive. I didn't want commitment, I didn't want a relationship. But I did want him to spend those two days in bed with me.

The coach stopped for a twenty-minute break. We got off and wandered down to the river. I totally lost track of time. Greg seemed just as besotted with me. We talked about music, travelling, films – everything except sex. But the chemistry between us was explosive.

Twenty minutes turned into an hour. When I realised the time, we ran back to the coach. Too late. It had gone – and taken Greg's bag with it. Greg was really panicking. I took charge. Luckily, we'd stopped by a hotel, so I phoned the coach company from there. They promised to hold onto it for him. Even luckier, a couple overheard us and offered us a lift into town.

They dropped us at my flat. I invited him in. At the time, I didn't even think what a risk I was taking – he was a total stranger, after all. We had a glass of wine. He took a shower and came out wrapped in my bath towel. I wanted him right then. But I had a shower too, then said, 'Let's go to bed.' He gave me a big, cheeky smile. It felt totally natural.

He led me into the bedroom, took off my towel and laid me on the bed. Then he stroked and kissed every part of me. I knew there was no way we'd start a relationship – he was leaving in two days, anyway – so I was totally uninhibited. I'd never been in that position – no hassle, no expectations, no future, just *now*. I showed him exactly how to touch me and bring me to orgasm. He did what I wanted. I took the lead, acting out everything in my fantasies – every position, every lick. It was better than the fantasy. When I looked down at him touching me, I couldn't believe it was happening. We took our time. I orgasmed as he gave me oral sex, and it was the most intense sensation I've ever felt.

We made love immediately afterwards, and by the time he'd orgasmed, I was ready to start again. For the next 48 hours, we stayed in bed, stroking, kissing, masturbating, making love, dozing – with the odd trip to the fridge in between. Time was limited, so we didn't want to stop! I orgasmed at least eight times. I'd never felt so uninhibited, so I'd never had orgasms like it. When I came, I really came!

The last couple of hours were tough. I knew he'd have to leave to collect his bag and catch his plane. I didn't want it to end. He gave me his home address and number in Australia, and said, 'Maybe I'll see you out there some day.' But we both knew it wouldn't happen. I did get a postcard from him in India a couple of months later.

Afterwards, I couldn't believe I'd taken such a risk. He was a total stranger. But it certainly isn't every day you get the chance to live out your fantasies – especially with the man you've fantasised about.

Tammy, 26

She confesses (boy–girl)

We had a 36-hour sex session – and I still don't know his name

For Julie, the urge to turn her on-line fantasies into reality was irresistible . . .

When I landed a new job with a design company in London, I thought I was ready for anything. But I never dreamed I'd end up having sex over the Internet.

I was single and full of ideas about what my new life in London would be like. Finding a flat was easy enough, and as I travelled to work on my first day, I really thought I'd made it. But after a week, the reality of moving to a big city hit home. I missed my friends and my old flat, and felt I didn't fit in.

Back home, I'd been outgoing and confident, but in unfamiliar London, I was self-conscious, even shy. Most of my colleagues at work were married with children and didn't have the time or money for socialising. The younger ones were trendy and stand-offish. I was lonely. So I started chatting to people on the Internet.

We had a PC with an Internet link in the far corner of our open-plan office. One night, I stayed on after work to send my family an email. It was a miserable night, and I didn't fancy going back to my flat, so I surfed around and went into a chat room. I called myself Roxanne.

Chatting quickly became an addiction. It was my entire social life. I often stayed late after work 'to do some research'. Shy, homesick Julie who didn't feel brave enough to go to the pub gave way to confident Roxanne. On the Net, I could be who I wanted. I met all kinds of people. Sometimes guys tried to talk dirty, but I wasn't interested. The idea of swapping dirty words did nothing for me.

One night, when none of my new friends were on line, a guy calling himself Rocco sent me a private message. It read, 'Wanna have some fun, Roxanne?' I was slightly intrigued so I replied, 'I doubt anything you could say would be fun.' He wrote, 'Perhaps nothing I could say, but something I could do.'

His words sent a shiver of excitement right through me. I'd been in London for two months and I hadn't been with any guys. I missed sex, but being turned on by a few words typed by a complete stranger made me feel like a totally sad case. I told myself he was probably an old, horribly ugly weirdo, but as he described 'tracing the outline' of my lips with his fingers and giving me a kiss deep enough to make me forget the rest of the world, I felt myself getting very wet.

I looked around the office, red faced and guilty, worried that someone would know my dirty secret. There were still a few people around, but no one was watching me. I squirmed a little on the chair, trying to squeeze my clitoris without touching it. I longed to masturbate.

We chatted for almost an hour. The more we chatted, the more I was turned on. I didn't actually come, but I was very, very close to it. By the end I was very wet. If I'd been able to touch myself, I would have orgasmed straight away.

I logged off and sat in the chair for a while to calm down. When I got home, I was too embarrassed and ashamed to masturbate. Being turned on by a stranger was just as bad as men watching porn or going to peep-shows – it was second-rate sex. I swore I wouldn't do it again. But the next night, after work, I logged on, telling myself it was 'just to see if he's there'.

He was. This time, he described making love to me on a clifftop with the sound of the sea below. We talked about exactly what we would do to each other. The thought of the other people in the office getting on with their work while I was on the verge of orgasm excited me even more. But afterwards I was still ashamed.

Over the next two weeks, we chatted most nights. I couldn't stop myself. Our fantasies ran wild. We 'made love' in a secret cave, in the ruins of a Roman temple, even on Concorde. But we never swapped personal details. When we chatted, I imagined him as Hugh Grant or Richard Gere. Sometimes I did long to know more, and I asked, but he'd type, 'Let's not get too personal.' All I knew was that he was 37, worked in finance, and lived somewhere in England.

One night, Rocco asked for my phone number. I was wary, but I did give it to him, and he called later that night. I was expecting him to sound like a dirty old man and destroy my fantasies for ever, but his voice was deep and sexy. He said my voice turned him on too, and we tried to make sense of the unbelievable sexual attraction between us. Then he talked about touching me. This time, alone in my flat, I could masturbate as he talked. After two weeks of pent-up sexual tension, my orgasm was pretty wild. I'd never had phone sex before, but it was amazing. Yet deep down, I still hated myself for having sex with a stranger. It was worse than a one-night stand. I didn't even know what he looked like.

Rocco rang me every night, and every night we had phone sex. Then he asked if I wanted to meet him in person and 'live this to the extreme'. I said yes, and we fixed a date for two weeks' time. He made it clear there was no commitment, no relationship, just sex. When I woke up the next morning, I was horrified by the idea. I didn't know anything about him, not even his real name. How could I have sex with him? Until now I'd masturbated – but this was different. And what if he was a psychopath?

Over the next two weeks, I went through every emotion imaginable – fear, apprehension, guilt, euphoria, excitement, terror, shame. But things had gone so far that I had to know who he was. I think I was also secretly hoping we might even form a relationship.

We met in a hotel bar. The place was pretty empty and I spotted him straight away. He'd described himself quite well, though my first thought was that he wasn't very good-looking. But he wasn't unattractive either. We had a drink and then went up to our room. He made it clear that we were here to act out our fantasies and that there was no question of a relationship. I went along with that, though deep down I was disappointed.

For the next 36 hours, I had the best sex I've ever had, stopping only for meals by room service, sleep or watching a bit of TV. I wasn't embarrassed at all – I was acting out my role as Roxanne. I did try asking about him but he wouldn't give anything away, so my guess is that he was married.

When we checked out, we shared a cab to the station. We were both quite embarrassed when we said goodbye on the platform, knowing that we wouldn't see each other again. Back at work, I did log on a few times, just to see if he was on line. Sometimes he was, but I didn't go into the chat room to speak to him. I did feel sad that whatever was between us had finished.

It was an extraordinary experience and one I'm so ashamed of that I haven't shared it with anyone – except *Cosmo*. After my night with him, I realised I had to sort my life out. I started socialising more and now I'm dating a guy from the office. It's great to have a proper, real relationship, but I'll never forget the thrill of cybersex.

Julie, 27

7
Planes, Trains and Automobiles

Why keep sex in the bedroom when there's the Mile High Club just waiting for you to join? From the top of the Eiffel Tower to the Eurostar train and the back of the number 32 bus, our saucy readers know just how to make their journey go with a bang.

It's not only the passengers who are up for it, either. Meet the two sexy stewardesses who get their kicks en route and the traffic warden who gives out more than parking tickets. But not everyone gets away with it . . .

She confesses (boy–girl)

I had sex with a stranger – at 32,000 feet

When he touched her in the darkness, Tamsin, the flight attendant, was too aroused to say no . . .

It had been the flight from hell. Twelve hours from London to LA, and a moaning passenger every minute. The cabin's too hot, the cabin's too cold, we don't like the food, there's not enough leg-room – I'd heard it all before. They even asked me to stop the turbulence. So by the time I crawled into my crew bunk for a rest, steamy sex was the last thing I expected.

Don't get me wrong, I enjoy working with passengers. Most of them, anyway. Without passengers, I wouldn't have a job.

But this was one flight too many. I'd been working non-stop for a month, taking only minimum rest breaks between flights. By the time I boarded the LA-bound Jumbo, each trip was blurring into the next. Then I was assigned to economy. I knew it would be a long haul in more ways than one.

I noticed him instantly. The single guy in 34F. Very Brad Pitt. He had to be American, with short blond hair, piercing blue eyes, jeans and a T-shirt. Late twenties, at a guess. He ordered a gin and tonic, with lots of ice, in a gorgeous Californian accent. Flirting was definitely out. In my job, you have to be professional. But at least having a few good-looking single guys on board makes the flight more exciting.

We served drinks and the first meal before the turbulence started. It wasn't bad, just enough to make a few passengers turn green. Not Brad. I asked if he'd like more coffee. He looked up from his copy of *GQ*, held up his cup and gave me a smile that had 'sex' written all over it. I'm used to appearing calm and in charge on the aircraft, but his look was so blatant that I couldn't help giving him a sexy smile back.

Clearing up sickbags soon took my mind off him. Four hours into the flight, my number one (the senior flight attendant) told me to take a two-hour break. I walked past 34F and noticed Brad wasn't in his seat. By the time I reached our crew bunks on the top deck, I was so tired that my eyes were half closed.

The crew rest area is a tiny room with four bunk beds, pyjamas and blankets. I didn't even bother to turn the light on. I'd seen the crew in business and first class, so I knew no one else was on a break. All I wanted to do was peel off my uniform and M&S support tights, crawl into the bunk and get some much needed sleep.

I was dozing when I heard a noise. It sounded like heavy breathing. At first I dismissed it as cabin noise. Then I heard it again. Someone was moving about in the bunk above me. I knew what had happened. There are always lots of airline staff on our flights, usually off-duty cabin crew going on holiday. One of them had obviously sneaked up here for a lie down. I was too tired to get involved, and it was too dark to see anything, so I dozed. But the noise kept me awake. The heavy breathing got louder and more rhythmic, and I heard groans too. They were certainly enjoying themselves. Was it one person masturbating, or was it a couple making love? I couldn't be sure. Whoever it was, I was incredibly turned on. Then I remembered Brad in 34F. He wasn't in his seat. Surely it wasn't him? Did he know someone in first class? Could he have sneaked up here?

My hand automatically slid down between my legs and I fingered my clitoris, fantasising that Brad was masturbating above me. Maybe I was too loud. I thought they'd be too busy to notice, but whoever it was climbed down from the top bunk and slid into bed next to me.

I was so engrossed in my fantasy that I pulled the man towards me. If he'd felt revolting, or was smelly, I'm sure I would have got out of bed. But he felt gorgeous. He had short hair, like Brad's, and a toned body. We kissed each other hard on the mouth and he stroked my clitoris faster and faster, while rubbing an ice cube on my nipples. His erection was subsiding, so I knew he'd reached orgasm before he got in bed with me, but that suited me fine. All I had to think about was myself.

He licked and stroked my nipples and clitoris while I fantasised he was Brad. As the ice cube melted, it trickled down my body, making me shiver with pleasure. Being touched by a stranger in the darkness was so incredible that I didn't want to orgasm – I wanted it to go on for ever – but I couldn't stop myself. When I came, it was so intense that I felt it in every muscle of my body. He climbed back into the top bunk without saying a word.

I was so relaxed and so warm that I fell asleep. The next thing I knew, my alarm was going off. What if he was still up there?

But I sensed the top bunk was empty. Someone was asleep in the other bottom bunk, though.

There was no choice. I couldn't hide in the rest area for ever. So I turned on the light. Mary, from business class, was snoring peacefully. It definitely hadn't been her.

I got dressed, freshened my make-up, and wondered how the hell I was going to face everyone, not knowing if I'd just had sex with them. I tried to remember if I'd seen every one of the sixteen crew before I went into the rest area, but I couldn't be sure. Did whoever it was know they'd had sex with *me*?

No one in business or first class batted an eyelid as I walked past them. Then came the long walk back to economy. I gave everyone a brisk smile as I passed. No one made eye contact. The crew were preparing another round with the drinks trolley, so I took Brad's aisle. I had to know if it was him.

Brad was still reading *GQ*. I was businesslike. 'Would you like a drink, sir?' He smiled, the same come-to-bed smile I'd seen earlier, and replied, 'A gin and tonic please, with lots of ice. The British don't like ice, do they?'

I still don't know for sure if I had sex with him, but there was something about his grin which told me I just might have.

Tamsin, 26

He confesses (boy–girl)

I had sex on Eurostar

When Andrew went to Brussels on a business trip, sex was the last thing on his mind. Then he met Sarah . . .

Getting up to catch the early morning Eurostar nearly killed me.

My hangover was pounding. I'd been out the night before with a couple of guys from work. You know the deal – just a quick drink. Eight pints later and we'd solved Third World debt. I wanted to sleep all the way to Brussels. So sex was the last thing on my mind, for once. Incredible sex in the Eurostar loo was definitely not on the agenda.

The train was almost empty. A couple of other guys in suits, obviously hungover too. A woman with a laptop, across the aisle. I stretched out over two seats and tried to get comfortable, but she was typing too loudly. Every tap was like a nail in the head. I figured I'd switch to another carriage.

I gave her a filthy look as I sat up. I wanted her to realise she'd bothered me. It turned into a smile. She was gorgeous. Long blonde hair, huge eyes, very Ally McBeal. Sexy suit, too. She smiled back. I hoped I didn't stink of stale booze. No way was I changing carriages now.

She carried on typing. I made some pathetic comment about working hard, but it got us chatting. The other two suits gave me 'you lucky bastard' looks. They didn't know how lucky I was going to get.

We flirted. She had a copy of *Cosmo*. We joked about it being 'full of sex'. That got us on the subject. Suddenly everything we said had a double meaning. I wanted her. It was a real animal attraction – I was semi-hard just talking to her. Sex was now back where it usually was – right at the front of my mind. I had a girlfriend. I always looked, sometimes flirted, but never touched. Until then.

She wanted a coffee from the buffet car, so I said I'd go too. She stood up. Her body was amazing – pert breasts, toned bum, tiny hips. I imagined touching her, being inside her. I often do that with women. – most guys do. But I didn't think it would happen, let alone three minutes later.

As we passed the loo, between carriages, I joked that there was probably a couple inside fulfilling their fantasies. She stopped walking, turned to me with a real wide-eyed look and asked if I'd ever wanted to have sex on a train. This was leading somewhere, but I couldn't quite believe it. I leaned against the loo door. I said it was my fantasy. It wasn't strictly true, but if this was heading where I thought it was, I had to show I was up for it. She smiled, reached behind me and opened the door. I backed in and pulled her in with me.

Inside, she bolted the door and giggled. It was as if she'd come this far and didn't know what to do next. I took over. I put my arms round her and we kissed, harder and harder. I slipped my hand inside her pants and stroked her clitoris. She was soaking. She pulled at my belt and said she wanted me inside her, now. I knew I'd orgasm quickly, but she was pulling at my zip. I undid my trousers and lifted her up so her legs were wrapped round my waist, with her back against the door. Anyone walking past would have heard me thrusting heavily against it.

It was the fastest, most frenzied, amazing sex I've ever had. I told her I was going to come, and went to pull out so I could stroke her some more, but she pulled me back in and said she wanted me to come. I saw our reflection in the mirror. It was such a turn-on that I couldn't hold back any longer. I came very, very loudly. Then she pushed my head down, so I squatted and gave her oral sex. I masturbated her to orgasm with my finger.

We hugged each other for a while. That meant we didn't have to look at each other and feel even more embarrassed. I couldn't believe what we'd just done. I joked about 'hoping no one heard us' to clear the air and said I'd go to get us a coffee. When I got back to my seat with the coffees, she'd gone. So had her laptop, her bag, everything. The suits saw me with two coffees and gave me a 'bet you thought you'd scored there, bad luck' look. If only they knew.

She was on the train somewhere, but I knew why she'd disappeared. I saw her get off at a stop in France. She didn't look back. To be honest, it suited me too. I was feeling guilty.

My girlfriend trusted me on business trips. That's the only time I've let her down, though I've masturbated over it many times. I still don't know who it was with, or why I did it, but it rates as the most amazing sexual kick of my life. So far. Every time I get on Eurostar for another business trip, I scan the carriage, just in case . . .

Andrew, 31

She confesses (boy–girl)

I had sex on the Number 32

They smiled at each other on the bus every day – then Sally invited him up to the top deck . . .

He was tall, blond and on my bus to work every morning. Very Brad Pitt – smart, with a hint of rebel. The type you just know will be fantastic in bed. So did I grab my chance? Flirt shamelessly and ask him out? I did more than that – I took him up to the top deck and had sex on the back seat. Why not? The upstairs was deserted, no one would ever know, would they? Oh yes they would. I'd forgotten the driver has an upstairs mirror. So, having got off, I went to get off – and suffered the most embarrassing experience of my life . . .

I still cringe when I talk about it. Sure, I've had great sex in some great places, but always with boyfriends. I'm not usually this shameful! But, to my credit, it did take two weeks of pretending not to look at each other on the bus every morning before we finally got to chat. The trouble was, once we spoke, that was it. I wanted him, right there, right then, on the bus. So I went for it – and gave the driver the sex show of his life.

I'd been catching that bus to work for a year. My two-woman company had a cleaning contract with a local office. Shift work wasn't ideal, but I was my own boss and it did mean stress-free commuting at 6 a.m. when almost everyone else was in bed. I saw the same few faces get on and off the bus each morning. It was usually the same driver, too. Being so early, people tended to nod to each other. Two hours later, I bet that bus was full of people in full-on commuter mode, desperately avoiding eye contact. But at 6 a.m. we were a friendly bunch.

The first morning he got on, I had a God-awful hangover and was wearing my oldest, grubbiest jeans and a faded T-shirt. I'd been single – and sex-free – for months. Even so, at 6 a.m. sex was the last thing on my mind. Then I saw him, and I couldn't stop thinking about it.

I sized him up while he was paying the driver. Smart suit, very sexy, but what really did it for me was his slightly too long blond hair and goatee. A hint of rebel. Perfect. Then he walked down the bus and sat in front of me. I shoved my nose in a book and hoped I wasn't radiating neat alcohol. Tomorrow, I promised myself, I'll wear something gorgeous and change at work.

He was still on the bus when I got off. I didn't pick up any vibes from him at all. He probably didn't even notice me. But he sure noticed me the next day. Cropped top, sexy jeans – I'd even got up at 5 a.m. to blow-dry my hair. I told myself I was mad, that he wouldn't even get on the bus again, but he did. We caught each other's eye and he gave me a half-smile, the kind that says, 'Wow'. Then he sat down behind me and I felt his eyes undressing me. It was such a turn-on. He sat there for ten minutes. Just the thought of him was making me wet. When the doors opened at my stop, I glanced back up the bus. He gave me a sexy look as I jumped off.

After two weeks of it, I was masturbating over him every night and getting pretty frustrated. I had to do something. So when he got on the bus the next day, I looked up and smiled. He took the hint, and sat down next to me.

The conversation turned smutty almost straight away. He asked which clubs I went to. One had recently held a fetish show – all leather outfits and whips – and he asked if I'd seen it. We went downhill from there, and I loved it. The last time I'd flirted on a bus, I was about fifteen. We were giggling like a couple of teenagers. Then he joked about 'shagging on the back seat'. We'd been chatting for about ten minutes. I was so horny that I grabbed his hand and said, 'Let's go upstairs.' I still don't know what came over me.

He chased me up the stairs and we fell on the back seats, still giggling. Then he kissed me. Luckily, the top deck was empty. I kissed him back, hard, and he shoved his hand up my top. I liked that – we were acting like teenagers, and that's how I wanted this sex to be – fumbly, quick and exciting. I undid his trousers and masturbated him roughly. Then I pushed him back down on the seat, climbed on top, and pushed my knickers to one side under my skirt so he could get inside me.

The bus jolted to a halt and I realised we were at a stop. Neither of us moved – we just stared down the aisle at the top of the staircase, praying no one would get on. They didn't. I reckoned we had about two or three minutes until the next stop, so I pushed my hand between us and masturbated quickly as we had sex. We came together, just as the bus pulled up for a second time.

I climbed off him and we sat next to each other, giggling. My knees were very sore because the seat was so scratchy, so I hate to think how his bottom felt. We did up our clothes and I suddenly realised I'd missed my stop. I wasn't worried about swapping phone numbers – I knew he'd be on the bus again tomorrow. So I grabbed my bag, ran down the stairs and rang the bell. He stayed upstairs.

At the next stop, the driver didn't open the doors. I stood there, wondering if they were jammed. Then he leaned out of his cab and shouted down the bus, 'I saw what you were doing up there. It's disgusting. I won't tolerate that kind of behaviour on my bus and I never want to see you on here again.'

I was utterly mortified. The worst of it was that everyone on the bottom deck – who I'd seen and nodded to hundreds of times – stared at me in disbelief. I didn't know what to say, where to look – or what they thought I'd been doing up there. The driver mumbled something about me being 'ashamed of myself' and finally opened the doors. I got off and ran back down the road, too embarrassed to look back.

I couldn't face ever getting on that bus again, but I have seen him since, at a couple of clubs in town. We smile, but nothing more. When I got to work that day, I told my colleague. She thought it was hilarious, and eight months on, I can just about see the funny side. It was the most fun, thrilling sex I've ever had – but I'm still walking to work because of it!

Sally, 27

She confesses (girl–girl)

I was seduced by a sexy stewardess

When the plane hit the tarmac at Heathrow, Michelle and the stewardess were still having sex . . .

I almost missed the flight. A quick glass of sangria by the hotel pool turned into three. Going home was the last thing I felt like. My week in Barcelona had been the best of my life – fabulous food, culture, and plenty of beautiful men and women to look at. What more could a bisexual girl ask for? I found out on the flight home. The sexual treat of a lifetime was waiting for me on board . . .

My girlfriend Lisa and I needed a break from each other. After three years together, we were – let's be upfront about it – bored. Going nowhere. So I went to Barcelona and she headed for Rome, to give us time to think. I felt like a kid leaving home, insecure and alone without her. But freedom felt good, liberating – at first. Then I really missed her. By the end of the week, I'd stayed faithful – physically, not mentally, as those Spanish girls were something else! – and I knew I wanted Lisa.

I drained my third sangria and checked the time. Panic swept through me like a rash. The flight was due to leave in ninety minutes. I'd never make it. But I found a taxi, and the airport staff ran me down corridors and shoved me onto the plane. By the time I'd fastened my belt, we were rolling back. Talk about cutting it fine. The sweat was literally dripping off me. All I wanted was a long soak in an expensive bubble bath with a trashy romance saga. Lisa wasn't due back until tomorrow. The girlie in me was fighting to get out. Twenty minutes later, she was out in full force . . .

The plane wasn't full, so I stretched out across the seats and tried to sleep, but I was far too hot and sticky. That's when I felt a gentle touch on my wrist. I opened my eyes and stared straight into the brightest green eyes I'd ever seen. The stewardess asked if I'd like a drink.

Maybe I touched her hand for a second too long. Maybe 'bisexual' was written all over my face. I didn't see it in hers. She was totally professional, and gorgeous. Long dark hair, tied back, and bright red, kissable lips. Someone to fantasise about later. What I really wanted was to freshen up and change. I remembered my holdall. There was a clean T-shirt and shorts right on the top. After lugging the bloody thing onto the plane, I might as well make use of it. The aircraft loo was too cramped to change in. Was there anywhere else I could do that?

She led me down the back of the plane to the crew quarters – a tiny room with lockers and a washbasin. I locked the door behind me, took off my jacket and top and leaned forward to wash my hands and arms. That's when I felt hands sliding round my waist. I was terrified. What kind of psycho would attack someone on a plane? I grabbed my deodorant and was about to turn around and squirt it in their face when I saw the nails. They were painted bright red. This was a woman. I stood up and looked in the mirror. The stewardess was behind me, smiling. She said, 'Is this OK?' in a Spanish accent. I nodded. OK? That was the understatement of the year.

I couldn't believe what a risk she'd taken. If I'd said no and reported her, that would have been the end of her career. How the hell she'd opened the door I don't know. I guess no aircraft door is totally stewardess-proof. Did the cabin crew know what she was up to?

She slipped off her jacket, pulled her top over her head and undid her bra. I couldn't believe my luck. After a week without sex, this was heaven. I felt guilty, but I couldn't say no. I took her breasts in my mouth and sucked them, pinning her against the door. I didn't understand what she was saying, but I was sure she liked it.

I reached under her skirt, slid my fingers inside her tights and knickers and stroked her clitoris. My nails were very long, so I was careful not to hurt her. She did the same. We masturbated each other, looking into each other's eyes. Feeling her push against my finger, moving up and down, was sensational. My whole body was shaking with pleasure, and I had to orgasm. As I came, she slipped her finger inside me, and came too, pretty loudly. I didn't want to stop, so I stroked and kissed her.

The next hour was total bliss. I jammed myself against the door so there was no way it could open. The cabin crew were bound to come looking for her. We kissed and masturbated each other, and took it in turns to give each other oral sex. We were still having sex when the plane began its descent. She masturbated me to orgasm for the second time just before we hit the tarmac.

The jolt knocked us both to the floor. I rubbed her clitoris until she came again. When the aircraft stopped, we were both still on the floor, surrounded by clothes, skirts around our waists. It was pure ecstasy.

I heard the other passengers leaving the plane, so I got dressed quickly, feeling hotter, stickier and luckier than ever. She pulled on her jacket and I noticed her name badge. Sex first, names later. When it's that good, why the hell not? She still doesn't know mine.

When I opened the door, the captain was standing at the end of the aisle. He winked at me as I passed, so I winked back. A couple of the other cabin crew grinned at me. They knew damn well what we'd been doing. Maybe she often did it. I prayed I'd get on one of her flights again.

I stuffed my track suit and toiletries back in my suitcase, got off the plane and freshened up as best I could in the loos by baggage reclaim. Lucky I did, because Lisa was there to meet me. She'd come home early. If I smelled of sex, she didn't notice. But I had to fake my orgasm with her that night. Joining the Mile High Club twice was enough for one day.

Michelle, 31

He confesses (boy–girl)

We had sex at the top of the Eiffel Tower

Stephen booked a romantic weekend in Paris with his girlfriend to make her fantasy come true . . .

Ellie told me about it on our second date. Over dinner. I started it. Ellie was a slim, bronzed brunette with skin you just had to touch. I thought if we got down to a sexually charged conversation, we'd end up in bed. It worked. After a few glasses of wine, we were swapping fantasies. Sex on the top of the Eiffel Tower. That was her big fantasy. She'd always wanted to do it. She'd been to Paris on a crazy weekend with the girls. She'd even met a guy out there, but it hadn't happened.

I toned my fantasies down, of course. Kept my desire to try sex with a prostitute to myself. I didn't think it would go down too well on a second date. I wouldn't do it, of course. It's one of those fantasies you know you'll never act out. But the Eiffel Tower – why not? I did confess to wanting oral sex under a restaurant table. She smiled, slid her hand across and stroked my balls. It drove me wild. I was already hard from hearing her fantasies. I pulled £60 out of my wallet, dropped it on the table and we left.

We had sex in my hallway, on the sofa, the kitchen floor and finally the bed. I came four times. She gave the best oral sex I've ever had. At work, I couldn't think about anything else. Our secretary had a plastic Eiffel Tower on her desk that snowed when you shook it. How phallic is that? Ellie's fantasy had me hooked. When I masturbated, I imagined having sex with her on top of the Eiffel Tower.

I liked her. Not just for sex – I really liked her a lot. Didn't want to push it. Would a weekend in Paris scare her off? What the hell. I called and asked if she wanted to go. Threw in some joke about the Eiffel Tower. She said yes, so I booked it. Then I wondered how the hell we'd have sex surrounded by tourists. That would spice up a few Japanese holiday videos.

I told my mates. Ever met a bloke who didn't? He's lying. I felt nervous on the plane, so I stuck to jokes about the Eiffel Tower to keep it light-hearted. We spent the first day in bed – we just couldn't get enough of each other, so we didn't see much of Paris. The next day, we promised each other we'd go sightseeing after breakfast. Both of us knew where we were heading – to the Eiffel Tower.

She was nervous too. Giggled a lot. We didn't mention sex. The Tower was packed, and freezing cold. The last place you'd want sex, to be honest. We made our way to the top after waiting ages for the lifts. It was worth it, though. The view was incredible. I stood behind her and hugged her, looking out at Montmartre. There was no way we could have sex up there.

Then she slid my hand down between her legs, and wrapped her coat tightly round her. From the back, it looked like we were just hugging. Then she slid in her opposite hand and unzipped her jeans.

I felt a wave of panic. What if I couldn't bring her to orgasm? We'd had a lot of sex, but I didn't know what she really liked. This would have to be quick, too. I slid my fingers between her legs. They were freezing, but she was warm and wet. It was a real turn-on for me too.

I stroked her clitoris, although I was too fast at first. She told me to slow down. Slowly and gently. Her breathing speeded up and she closed her eyes. I glanced around. No one was taking any notice, thank God. I was so hard I couldn't stop myself pushing my penis into her back.

She was on the verge of orgasm when a group of German tourists crowded next to us. I heard her say 'Oh God' and begin to shudder. The tourists looked round. Still masturbating her, I faked a coughing fit, covering my mouth with my other hand. I couldn't think of anything else. They looked away. She came pretty hard, then we both burst out laughing. We couldn't believe we'd done it.

I was so horny, I wanted to burst. It didn't subside even while we waited for the lifts down. I bought her a snowing Eiffel Tower as a memento, then we went straight back to the hotel and had sex. Making her fantasy come true made me feel so good.

Our relationship lasted two years. Sex was fever pitch for

most of that. We tried staying friends when it ended, but we fancy each other too much for it to work. Last time I saw her, the plastic Eiffel Tower was still on her mantelpiece. I get a kick when I think of her new boyfriends maybe picking it up, shaking it – and not knowing what we did up there.

Stephen, 32

He confesses (boy–girl)

She gave me more than a parking ticket

When Andy left his car on a double yellow line, he wasn't expecting any sexual favours . . .

I was late – bloody late. The M25 was one big circular car park. I put the roof down on the BMW before my stress levels went right through it. This was one meeting I didn't want to miss. Our PR firm wanted these new clients. Make that needed. My job was to sign them up. So when I pulled up outside, ten minutes after my presentation should have started, I didn't give a toss about the double yellow lines. If I nailed the deal, a parking ticket would be worth it. It turned out to be worth it in more ways than one . . .

They wouldn't commit, of course. Said they'd 'be in touch'. To be honest, turning up late wasn't impressive. It was all my girlfriend's fault. She'd decided to climb on top of me just as I was getting out of bed. Of course, I wasn't going to say no. Half an hour – and some great sex – later, I finally made it to the shower – and then hit the M25 in the rush hour. Now it might turn out to be a wasted journey anyway. So I wasn't in the best of moods when I crashed through the revolving doors and back out to my car. And guess what? A bloody traffic warden was sticking a ticket on it.

I know what you're thinking. I stormed over, had a massive row and we ended up having rough, raw sex, right? Totally wrong. OK, I admit I felt like yelling at her – or worse – but there was still a chance the company would sign us up, and I didn't think it would do much for our image if they looked out of the window and saw their future PR man ranting like a lunatic. So I took the 'quietly seething' approach. I walked up to the car, pointedly ripped the ticket off the windscreen and stared at it. She was fiddling about with a hand-held ticketing machine. I glanced up, ready to give her my best filthy look, and realised she was absolutely bloody gorgeous. It hadn't even occured to me that she'd be beautiful. I was expecting Margaret Thatcher. So what did I do? Did I scowl? Did I look furious? Did I hell. I smiled.

She was one of those girls who look incredible in anything. Short blonde bob, sexy eyes, cute turned-up nose and what looked like a very gorgeous body underneath the white shirt and dark trousers. She grinned back. I don't normally have trouble chatting up women, but the fact she was a traffic warden totally threw me. The last time I felt anything like it, I was about thirteen and being ticked off by our stunning English teacher.

I couldn't think of a word to say. I stood there grinning at her like a bloody Cheshire cat. She realised the effect she was having on me. I'm sure that sense of power really turned her on, because she started flirting. She ran her fingers along the car and said, 'Nice BMW.' Believe me, most guys love their 'boys' toys', and having them praised – and stroked – by a woman gives you a real kick. It's the next best thing to sex. I never dreamed I had that coming, too . . .

We didn't waste time with chit-chat. The flirting, the innuendoes, were the full-on, in-your-face type. You know, what did I get up to behind my tinted windows, that kind of thing. I wasn't sure where this was heading, but I sure as hell wasn't going to stop. I've never experienced sexual attraction like it. This was pure animal lust. Just looking at her was making me hard, and I sensed she was feeling the same. Trust me, when a guy chats to a woman he fancies, he imagines her naked. That's what I was doing, and it was turning me on. I thought maybe I'd get her number, if I was lucky.

She said I'd better move the car, or it might be towed away. So I asked her where to park. She pointed round the corner and gave me directions to a quiet road just a couple of hundred yards away. Then she bent down by my window and said, 'I'll meet you there.'

I didn't think for a second that she'd turn up. But I drove to the road anyway. It was a quiet backstreet with loads of spare parking meters. I put some cash in the meter, then sat there with my windows shut and radio on, feeling, if I'm honest, pretty stupid – and expecting to appear on some future episode of *Trigger Happy TV*. 'The Sad Guy Who Thought A Stunning Traffic Warden Wanted Sex With Him'. But then there was a tap on my passenger window, and she got in.

We didn't say a word, we just kissed. My hands were all over her. Normally I take things slow, but I couldn't hold back. She was the same. I undid her shirt and kissed her breasts. The whole 'schoolmistress' thing – even though she wasn't one – was turning me on. She reached down, pulled off her trousers and masturbated herself. Then she pushed my head down between her legs and I gave her oral sex, masturbating myself at the same time. I just couldn't believe my luck. I still can't.

I tipped my seat right back and she climbed on top of me. It was pretty squashed, but we had very fast, very hot and very sticky sex right there on the driver's seat. She masturbated too, and when I felt her orgasm, I came very hard and far too loudly. We both started laughing.

She climbed off, back into the passenger seat, and put her

clothes back on, still giggling. Thank God for tinted windows, though I couldn't help feeling that someone must have seen – or heard – us. There was a guy on his mobile phone up the far end of the street, but he wasn't taking any notice. I said something like, 'I don't suppose you'll let me off the ticket?' and she reached down on the floor, picked up her ticketing machine and said, 'Sorry, I can't. It's on here.'

Of course, that wasn't the version I told my mates. They all think I impressed her with my flashy car, gave her fantastic sex and got away with being given a ticket. To be fair, she was the one in charge, the one giving the fantastic sex – and that's what really turned me on.

I didn't ask for her number and she didn't offer it – she just touched up her make-up in the passenger mirror, kissed me on the cheek, said, 'That was great,' then got out and walked off. I sat there for a while and had a cigarette, half hoping she'd come back, reliving the memory and enjoying every minute. Then I thought about my girlfriend, felt guilty, and frantically checked the car to make sure there were no earrings or other give-aways left in it. She never found out, and I don't plan on telling her. It was a one-lunchtime stand, pure sexual attraction, nothing more. OK, I shouldn't have done it. But, God, I'm glad I did.

We didn't land the PR contract, so I haven't been back to that part of town since. But I wouldn't want us to meet again anyway. What happened was an incredible one-off, and best left as that. I always look closely at traffic wardens, but I've never seen another one anywhere near as sexy as her.

Andy, 28

She confesses (boy–girl)

My Transatlantic triumph

Tessa's flights to the US always bored her stiff, until she took a trip to the heights of sexual ecstasy . . .

I saw him at check-in. Dark suit, white shirt, cute public-school haircut. Hugh Grant with attitude. There was apparently some mix-up on the tickets and business class was full. He wasn't having any of it. Ten minutes, three arguments and several polite threats later, he got what he wanted. He was the type that always does. Six hours later, we got what we wanted from each other. At 36,000 feet.

The eight-hour night flight home from the States usually bored me rigid. Sweaty, overweight businessmen for company and doses of plastic food every few hours. At least my flat was at the end of it. I had established a routine – a curt 'hello' to my neighbour, then earphones on to keep my distance. But this time was different. He was sitting in the window seat next to me.

I slid into my seat and smiled at him. He grinned back. There was no mistaking it – desire was written all over his face. The stewardess offered us a drink. G&T for me, vodka for him. We flirted. Had a few more drinks. He was 29, single and worked in advertising, like me. Pretty much a dream come true. Early on, he said we should swap numbers and go for a drink in London sometime. I was up for that. And more.

Three hours into the flight, they turned the lights down. I didn't put my reading light on. Neither did he. I pulled a blanket over me and closed my eyes. He was just inches away. I wanted him so badly. Slowly, I slid my head nearer and nearer to his shoulder. As it touched him, I thought he'd draw back, but he rested his head on mine.

My heart was pounding and I was breathing really quickly. It was the biggest turn-on of my life. Still pretending to be asleep, I slowly lifted my head up. He kissed me.

It started gently. Our lips just brushed. I wasn't even sure if it was a kiss. Then it got more and more passionate. I couldn't believe what I was doing. Knowing we couldn't move about or make a noise made the thrill even better. I was so wet and so close to orgasm that I had to have him touch me. I slid my hand under his blanket and over his penis. It was so hard that I knew he was close to orgasm too.

He sat back in his seat and I did the same. Then we masturbated each other under the blankets, all the time facing straight ahead, eyes closed, pretending to be asleep. He gave my clitoris long, slow strokes, then shorter and faster, shorter and faster, until I orgasmed. It was incredible. I tried not to shudder too much, but my orgasm was so intense that I couldn't help it. Luckily, the drone of the aircraft drowned out my gasps. After I came, I looked around guiltily, realising what I'd just done, but the other passengers seemed to be asleep. I hope they really were.

Masturbating him was more difficult. I had to use my left hand, and I was afraid someone would notice my arm pumping up and down. So I rested my head in his lap, lying on his penis. He groaned. I slipped my head under the blanket and gave him oral sex. From this position, I could use my right hand too, and as I stroked underneath his balls, he came. He was pretty quiet until he orgasmed, when he said, 'Oh my God' really loudly. To this day, I don't know if anyone looked round. I kept my head under the blanket.

When I sat up, he smiled at me and kissed me. I finished what was left of my fifth G&T, rested my head on his shoulder and dozed, at peace with the world.

Then the lights came on. Suddenly I was plunged back into reality. Stewards bustled round with breakfast trays, throwing open window shutters and talking about landing at Heathrow. I had a terrible headache, my make-up was a mess and I couldn't even look at him. I had given him a blow-job. What on earth did he think of me? I grabbed my bag and went to the loo to tidy myself up.

I thought he'd ignore me but he said, 'Breakfast is served,' with the kind of grin that told me everything was OK. We made small talk and then I blurted out, 'I can't believe what I did earlier.' He said, 'Nor can I, but I hope you'll come out for dinner with me this week,' and handed me a card with his work and home numbers on it. I was half expecting a girlfriend to meet him at the airport, but we walked to the taxi rank together and fixed up a date.

We dated for several months. It was hard not to laugh when people asked how we first met. The relationship started with a bang, but it gradually fizzled out. Sex was great, but it never touched the raw passion we felt on that plane.

Tessa, 29

8
Keep it in the Family

There's something super-sexy about people you shouldn't have sex with. Not your blood relatives, of course, but how about your best friend, your boyfriend's best friend, even his sister . . . Haven't you ever caught yourself fancying them just a teensy bit?

These naughty confessors had – but they didn't stop at fantasising. From the best man who has sex with the bride to the girl who gives her boyfriend's dad 'the best oral sex he's ever had', we get intimate with readers who just couldn't stay loyal – and find out just how incredible sex can be when you break all the rules.

He confesses (boy–girl)

I was the best man – in more ways than one

John knew he'd end up in bed with Lisa one day. But he didn't think it would happen on her wedding day . . .

Mike was the original commitment-phobe. Casual sex and quality lads' nights out were Mike's idea of a good time. Then he met Lisa. Talk about a U-turn. Within a year, I was best man at their wedding, taking care of the rings, giving the speech – and having sex with the bride round the back of the marquee.

Don't get me wrong, I'm not a total bastard. I still feel very guilty about what happened. Mike is my best mate. But I wanted Lisa from the day we met. I thought once they were married I'd shake it off. That's what I hoped, for my sake. But she looked so gorgeous in that wedding dress, and the sexual attraction between us just boiled over.

Mike first turned up with Lisa at a dinner party. Strolled in casually, said, 'Hi guys, this is Lisa,' and asked me how work was going. Perfectly normal behaviour, you might think. Not for Mike. He'd been single – and proud of it – for three years. Mike got plenty of casual sex. Sometimes he even saw a girl twice. But he never invited them to meet us, the 'inner circle', as he called us. Not until Lisa. He hadn't even mentioned her.

This had to be serious, and I could see why. Lisa was stunning. Mike and I always went for the same type of girl. The stereotyped tall, leggy blonde. Preferably with Eva Herzigova breasts. Sorry if that sounds laddish, but blondes just do it for me. Lisa had it all – and a Masters in psychology.

I didn't pick up any sexual vibes from her that first night, but when I got home I masturbated while thinking about her. Watching her over dinner – laughing, chatting, fingering the rim on her wine glass – had given me an erection. Being Mike's girlfriend made her untouchable – and even more desirable. But I didn't think we'd ever have sex.

Mike told me all about their incredible sex life. It turned me on just hearing about it. I told him I thought she was gorgeous, but Mike's far too confident to lose sleep over that. Make that arrogant. It wouldn't occur to him that Lisa might fancy me too. To be honest, it hadn't seriously occurred to me either – except in my dreams. He said Lisa gave the best oral sex he'd ever had, and each time I saw her, I imagined her doing that to me.

Then they announced their engagement. How did I take it? 'Congrats, well done', a slap on the back for Mike and a kiss on the cheek for Lisa. Inside, I was pretty devastated. Lisa and I had become close and I'd started to fancy my chances if they ever split up. It took me a few days to dump it all in the trash and move on. I started dating Kathy, a girl from work, and had plenty of sex to take my mind off it.

Then Mike sold his flat and moved in with me while the deal went through on their new place. That meant I saw Lisa almost every day. Sometimes Mike had gone to work, so we had breakfast together. She fancied me, I was sure of it. She didn't flirt, and neither did I, but when we looked at each other, you couldn't hide the sexual attraction. Was I pleased? Yeah, in a way. But my overwhelming thought was, 'Oh shit.' Their wedding was in two weeks. If only Lisa had let me know earlier. Now it was far too late to do anything about it. Or so I thought . . .

I started leaving for work early so I wasn't alone in the house with her. I didn't want to do anything I'd regret.

The wedding went like clockwork – big marquee, unlimited booze, unpronounceable French food. Mike never did anything by halves. When I saw Lisa walk up the aisle, I wished to God I was the groom, not the best man. She looked beautiful and sexy – and didn't make eye contact with me all through the service, even when I handed over the rings. Probably best, I decided. Nothing happened between us, nothing ever will. Time to move on.

I stayed sober until after my speech. Considering what a naughty boy Mike had been pre-Lisa, I let them off lightly on the anecdotes. Then I hit the bar, big time. Kathy was winding me up with hints about marriage. No chance. I needed to get very drunk. Luckily, I was only on my fourth Whisky Mac when Lisa came over and asked me if we could have a chat outside. She'd had a few drinks, but she wasn't drunk.

It was dark, and I didn't have a clue where we were going. This was her parents' garden, so I followed her. We stepped over most of the marquee guy ropes, then Lisa tripped, and I caught her. That started us giggling. She looked at me seductively and I knew she'd called me outside for sex.

Did I think about Mike? Yes. Did it stop me? No. Nothing could have stopped us, short of getting caught. We both wanted it badly. Lisa pulled me through a gap in the hedge and we fell onto the ground under some trees. The garden was lit, so I could see her pretty clearly. She was still wearing her wedding dress, and the live music was pumping out of the marquee. My hands were all over her. Touching Lisa felt so good, and knowing she wanted me so much that we were having sex on her wedding day just blew my mind. Her wedding dress, the fact this was 'wrong', and the risk of getting caught just turned me on even more. She pulled my braces and trousers down and ripped open my shirt, snapping the buttons. This was fast and furious. I pushed up her wedding dress and we masturbated each other roughly. Neither of us said a word. Lisa was very wet and pulled me on top of her. She wanted sex. I knew we had to be quick. When I slid inside her, with her dress jammed between us, I felt so excited that I almost came. Lisa rolled me on to my back and straddled me. Her wedding dress was all over my face and her fingers were frantically masturbating her clitoris. She came quickly, and as I felt her orgasm, I pushed deep inside her and came too.

Lisa rolled off me, her wedding dress covered in twigs and soil. Her hair had come undone too. She started giggling again and said, 'God, I needed that. We had to get that out of our systems, right?' By that, I guessed this was a one-off. I was stupid to think it was anything more. What else could it be? Then the guilt kicked in. I didn't want to get caught. What the hell could we do? There was no way we could go back to the reception in the state we were in.

Lisa had already thought of that. She said we could change in her bedroom. We sneaked back to the house and upstairs like a couple of kids. Everyone was in the marquee. Lisa found me an old shirt of her dad's. I went back to the party and put on my morning coat, in case Lisa's dad recognised the shirt. Kathy asked where I'd been. I faked a stomach bug and said we'd have to leave early.

When Lisa came back in, she'd changed into her evening dress. No one suspected a thing. We made eye contact and she grinned. I left the reception soon after, and persuaded Kathy to stay behind. I needed some space.

I didn't see Lisa again until after their honeymoon, and each time she's been with Mike. We've never mentioned it, but I see far less of them now because I don't want Mike to pick up on any vibes between us. The attraction is still there. I often fantasise about sex with Lisa, but I never did find out how good she is at oral sex. Maybe I will, one day.

John, 29

She confesses (girl–girl)

My lover found me in bed with my best friend

Millie had one of her most intense orgasms with her best friend Charlotte . . .

Jason and I had been together for a year, and our sex life was still as hot as ever. He knew exactly how to satisfy me. I loved experimenting with new positions and places, and though Jason didn't have my imagination, he was totally open to new ideas. I had my flat, a great job and a man I loved who was brilliant in bed – what more could I desire? Then I met Charlie, and suddenly all I wanted to do was have sex with her.

I'll never forget the first time I saw Charlie. She turned up at my flat with another friend. I noticed how attractive and sexy she was, just as any other straight woman would. As the evening wore on, we ended up talking intently to each other about life and our boyfriends. Face to face, my feelings towards her began to change. All I could think about was how beautiful she was, and how I wanted to touch her intimately and kiss her. Just looking at her turned me on.

By the time Charlie left, I was totally confused. I was straight, in love with Jason, and happy, so I could not understand why I was so aroused by her. Wanting sex with someone other than Jason made me feel guilty enough, but the fact I desperately wanted sex with a straight woman made me wonder if there was something 'wrong' with me. I'd never felt turned on like this by a woman before.

Over the next six months, Charlie and I became close friends. I introduced her to Jason and she joined our group. I found myself fantasising about her. We were an open, fun-loving group, and the girls often flirted with the guys, especially after a few drinks. One night, everyone was flirting outrageously as usual when Charlie looked at me with real 'come to bed' eyes. I pretended it was a bit of fun, and flirted back, egged on by all the men. But deep down I wasn't embarrassed, I was flattered. I wanted her so badly, and I had a feeling she wanted me too.

After that, it became an in-joke that Charlie and I would tease the boys with our 'two-woman fantasy', and our flirting escalated. So did my desire. Sometimes when we hugged goodbye, we'd hold onto each other just a few seconds longer, savouring it. Even though I loved Charlie as a friend, I didn't for a second imagine myself in a relationship with her. I just wanted her physically.

A few weeks later, Charlie and I had a girls' night in with a pizza and a bottle of wine. We were a bit drunk, and got talking about sex. Somehow we ended up on the idea of two women. Just talking about it with her turned me on. I asked Charlie if she'd ever been with another woman and she said no, but admitted she'd fantasised about it. Then she asked me. I said I'd never thought about it seriously. We quickly got the conversation back onto 'safe' subjects, but I think both of us knew after that night that it was only a matter of time . . .

One night, when Jason had gone to stay with his brother, Charlie and I went to the pub on our own. We often did that, and I didn't think, or plan, that this would be a special night. We had a lot to drink and when we got back to the flat, giggly, Charlie tripped over and fell onto my bed. I fell with her. We looked at each other and it just happened. It was the most passionate kiss I'd ever experienced. All those months of pent-up sexual tension came flooding out.

After that kiss, we slowly took off each other's clothes. There was no embarrassment, no rush, none of that raw energy you get on a fast one-night stand. We must have taken at least an hour and a half. We touched and stroked each other's skin and hair, and it was the most sensual experience imaginable. Everything felt so natural. We spent ages stroking each other, then I moved my hand down to Charlie's clitoris. At first I wasn't sure what to do. I felt as if I was taking the man's role. I'm sure Charlie felt the same. But I did what feels good for me, and Charlie liked it.

We didn't have any sex toys, but I didn't miss penetration. I like a man to be firm with me, but Charlie was very gentle, and it made the whole experience so different and exhilarating. I went down on her, and that was when she came. Afterwards, we spent a few minutes stroking and cuddling, then she went down on me. It was so much nicer than having oral sex from a man. Sometimes, when a man goes down on me, it's more irritating that pleasurable. But Charlie was spot on. When I orgasmed, it was intense. I don't think it was better than an orgasm with Jason, it was just different.

Afterwards we cuddled for a while, both totally relaxed and satisfied. Neither of us said it, but we both knew this was a one-night stand, something we just had to do. I've had a couple of one-night stands with men in the past, but this time there was no worrying about what someone thought of me, or whether they'd brag about it to their mates down the pub. I knew we were both in happy relationships and hadn't misled or hurt each other in any way.

I woke up the next morning when I heard the front door slam. Jason was home. He walked straight into the bedroom. Charlie and I were lying apart on either side of the bed. I could tell from Jason's face he assumed we'd just shared the bed after our night out. He smiled at me and quickly left the room, so as not to impose on Charlie's privacy. He looked so sweet. That's when I felt very confused about what I'd done. The night before, I hadn't felt that sleeping with Charlie was being unfaithful to him. I saw it as something different, something I needed to experience. But in the cold light of day, I realised Jason would see it as betrayal. Half of me felt that because it was with a woman, it didn't really count. The other half felt incredibly guilty, and I realised I'd jeopardised my relationship with him.

Charlie and I got up, dressed, and jokingly said, 'Thanks for last night,' the way blokes do. We both knew we'd got it out of our system. Our friendship was as strong as ever, though we didn't flirt after that night.

Over the next few days, my guilt worsened. I felt Jason had a right to know, and that if I didn't tell him, my secret might damage our relationship in the long run. I didn't like Charlie knowing something that Jason didn't. But I was too afraid he'd finish with me. Six months later, I almost told him, but I still couldn't risk losing him over it.

Two years on, Jason and I are still together and Charlie is still a close friend. Charlie and I haven't had sex with each other since, or wanted to. Sex between Jason and I is great, and I think we'll probably end up married. I do hate having a guilty secret, and my one wish is that I'd had sex with Charlie before I met him. Then I could have told him about it. But the intense sexual desire between me and Charlie was something that just had to be purged.

Millie, 27

He confesses (boy–girl)

I had sex with my father's girlfriend

When Mike slept with Sarah, he had no idea there was a family tie . . .

We're not talking Anne Bancroft. She was in her late twenties, gorgeous, and in my local club. How the hell was I supposed to know she was dating my father? Someone like Sarah could have anyone she wanted. She just happened to want my dad.

The odds have got to be millions to one against. Make that billions. I'm in Brighton, my dad's in London. Sure, he's good-looking. He hasn't even lost his hair. When Mum left him, Dad played the field. I saw him every couple of months, usually with a different woman. Then he met Sarah and told me it was serious. Then I met Sarah in a club – and unknowingly had sex with my future stepmother.

I almost didn't go to the club that night. God, I wish I hadn't. I'd organised a big sales presentation at work, so a couple of beers on the way home was enough for me. But two beers turned into four, then six, and I ended up in a cab with Fat Tony, my main sales rival, still wearing my suit. We were pretty loud outside the club. That's when I noticed her. Petite, blonde, very, very pretty – and looking at me.

We got chatting at the bar. I made the first move, but we'd made so much eye contact that I knew she wanted me to. She lived in London, worked in marketing and was visiting friends for the weekend. And yes, she had a serious boyfriend. That didn't bother me. It obviously wasn't serious enough to stop her chatting me up. It turned out we'd even been at uni in London at roughly the same time, though we'd never met. I was sure about that – I'd know her face anywhere.

I'll be honest – I wasn't looking for a relationship. I'd just split up with my girlfriend of four years. So Sarah was perfect. She had a boyfriend, lived miles away and, judging by the way she touched my hand as we chatted easily, wanted 'something for the weekend'.

She invited me back to her friends' flat. I'd had a lot to drink, but I remember getting into a cab with Sarah and two other girls. We all shared a couple of bottles of wine and watched MTV. Sarah curled up next to me. I realised she was sleeping on the sofa. I was so horny I almost told the other girls to go to bed. Or join in, I didn't care. When they finally went, Sarah turned and kissed me.

She was wearing this cute cropped top and jeans. I pushed my hands inside her top and massaged her breasts. They were small, so she wasn't wearing a bra, but that really turned me on. She unzipped my trousers and masturbated me so hard that I had to take her hand and slow it down. I didn't want to come too quickly.

After that, the sex was pretty slow and sensual. I slid down her jeans and we masturbated each other, then I gave her oral sex. She was gorgeous. I didn't realise she was so close to orgasm, but she suddenly let out a gasp and began to shudder. As her orgasm subsided, I slid her jeans off, climbed on top and went inside her. It was slow, intense and, when I came, I knew it was the best one-night stand I'd probably ever have.

We dozed on the sofa for a while, but by now it was light and I didn't fancy getting caught by her two mates with my trousers down, so I got dressed. Sarah was still asleep. I didn't want to sneak out, so I woke her up gently and said, 'Thanks for a great night.' OK, I admit it, I was half hoping she'd ask for my number. But she just gave me a sleepy smile.

Fat Tony wanted a blow-by-blow account on Monday morning. He got it. I'd masturbated over sex with Sarah all weekend. We even went back to the club the following Friday, but she wasn't there. Four months later, Sarah was a happy – but distant – memory.

I'd seen Dad a couple of times since that night. He mentioned his new girlfriend Sarah, and even said she was 'a bit younger', but we spent most of the time talking about football or work. Then he invited me to his place for dinner, to meet her. I decided I'd stay overnight.

Sarah was in the kitchen when I arrived. Dad took me into the living room and called, 'Sarah, Mike's here.'

I will never forget seeing her in the doorway. It's totally impossible to describe the shock. She went completely white. I'm sure I did, too. I was frantically trying to hold it together, but Dad realised straight away that something was up and said, 'Is everything all right?'

I couldn't even speak. Talk about useless. Sarah – who I guess had more to lose – was quicker thinking. She said, 'Weren't you at uni in London? Early nineties? What a coincidence. Long time no see.' Then Dad joked, 'Oh, not boyfriend and girlfriend, I hope?' He was half serious. We both laughed nervously. It couldn't get any worse.

I had to cover this up for Dad's sake. Knowing I'd slept with Sarah would totally destroy him. So I pulled myself together, played it cool and said, 'Oh, no, nothing like that.' Then I mumbled about Sarah knowing my ex-girlfriend.

We spent most of the evening talking about uni and not flirting in any way. I just wanted it to end. How did I feel? Angry that Sarah had betrayed my dad, worried that she did it often, jealous, if I'm truthful, that Dad was having sex with her.

Above all, I wished I hadn't.

I couldn't face staying the night. I said I had to help a friend move house on Sunday morning. The thought of Sarah and Dad in the room next to me was too much to handle. I stayed sober and drove home.

Sarah rang me at work on the Monday. I don't know how she got my number. She thanked me for keeping quiet about our one-night stand, and said she didn't make a habit of it, she just really fancied me. OK, I was flattered. Maybe she lied. Maybe she thought flattery would keep me quiet. But I'd never seen Dad so happy and I sure as hell wasn't going to spoil it.

I was in the States when they got married, a year later. 'Unavoidably detained on business.' I made damn sure I was. Since that phone call, Sarah and I have never mentioned it. My current girlfriend doesn't know either, and I'll never tell her. Nor have I told my mates. Too risky. I see Sarah and Dad occasionally, and they seem happy together, but I can't get the image of giving her oral sex out of my head.

Mike, 29

She confesses (boy–girl)

I had fantasic sex with my man's best friend

Helen's boyfriend was asleep in the next room, but that didn't stop her having her cake and eating it . . .

There's always 'one that got away'. You know, the guy you should have had sex with, or married, or both. Justin definitely fell into the 'sex' category. If I'd met him first, who knows what might have happened? But I didn't. I met Peter. So here I was, two years down the line, with a steady, good-looking, sincere boyfriend who bought me flowers, remembered my mother's birthday and – this is a classic – filed his bank statements in date order. And here I was, fantasising like crazy about Justin, a guy whose idea of fidelity was getting your name right during sex. Then, one night, we found ourselves alone in the kitchen. The mood was right, the chance was there and Peter was spark out in the bedroom next door. Was I going to sit back and wait for my ship to come in? Not bloody likely. This time I was rowing out to meet it.

Talk about chalk and cheese. If Justin and Peter hadn't grown up together as kids, they'd never have become friends. They were both good-looking, but in totally opposite ways. Girls went wild over Justin. He was so pretty that at first you assumed he was gay. Blue eyes, blond hair, a turned-up nose and an amazing ability to listen, so that when you talked he made you feel like the most special person in the world. It was a winning cocktail, and Justin knew it. Justin had girlfriend after girlfriend and was incredibly sweet to them all – for the few days they dated. A classic serial monogamist. Peter was tall, dark haired, and quieter. Handsome, not pretty. The type that usually wears a suit – even when casually dressed, you could picture him in one. I doubt Justin even owned a suit. He bowled up in the pub wearing surfing shorts, T-shirts and, as he worked as a garden designer, a gorgeous tan. To me, Justin breathed sex. He was so alive, so full of life, and Peter was so reserved and repressed. Peter meant stability, safety. Justin meant fun. We'd flirted with each other since the day Peter introduced us, but I didn't think things would ever go any further . . .

I'd known Peter for two weeks when we first met up with Justin. I'd heard all about him, of course, and Peter had said, with a resigned look, 'You're bound to fancy him. Everyone does.' He was right. Justin wasn't the type you want to marry or take home to mum and dad. But he was exactly the type you want to have sex with. Lots of sex, in lots of different places. I was careful not to flirt at first. But after a few weeks, our relationship settled down. We flirted, I teased him about his string of girlfriends, and Peter put up with it. As Peter pointed out once, at least if we were mucking around and flirting in front of him, there was nothing going on behind his back. There wasn't – until Peter's birthday . . .

I'm still ashamed when I talk about this. Of all the nights to be unfaithful, your boyfriend's thirtieth birthday isn't really one of them. But, trust me, it was worth it!

Peter and I had been together for two years, but the last three months hadn't been great. We'd hit that 'shall we get married or split up?' stage. Peter was 29 going on 40. He wanted to get married – working at the bank, he'd got a cheap mortgage, so he already owned a lovely house. And he thought I should move into it. I was 26 and I liked my flat, my independence. But I also loved Peter. The trouble was, we weren't 'in love' any more. Sex was fine, but bloody repetitive. I always came – we followed a well-rehearsed pattern! – but he wasn't up for experimenting. If I gave him the come-on in a hotel bar, or on the beach, he'd get embarrassed and suggest we go back to our room. So I was bored. I wanted someone who was even more up for it than I was. That's where Justin came in . . .

Peter's thirtieth bash turned into the birthday party from hell. We'd been arguing all week over stupid things, and I think we both knew it wasn't working, but with the party on Saturday, there was no way we could split up. Peter started drinking at lunchtime, and by the time everyone arrived at the pub for his party, he was completely plastered. Justin turned up on his own and when I asked where his latest girlfriend was, he said, 'I'm hoping to get lucky tonight.'

I honestly don't think he had any intention of making a move on me. But as he said it, we both looked at each other and something clicked for both of us. I'd never seen Justin embarrassed before, but he picked up the sudden sexual vibe between us and clearly didn't know what to do with it. We both stood there awkwardly – we'd never felt uncomfortable in each other's company before – and Justin said suddenly, 'I'd better get a drink.'

Usually, we'd have spent most of the party chatting together. But this time, Justin and I avoided each other, just catching each other's eye occasionally. There was no obvious come-on – this was a deeper, burning, more passionate desire. We hardly spoke all night, which was unusual, but I think we were both worried about where this was heading.

Peter was oblivious to everything. By the end of the party, he was so drunk that he couldn't stand up. Justin asked if I wanted a hand getting him home. So the three of us caught a taxi.

I can't even blame the drink – I'd had a few, but I wasn't that drunk. Neither was Justin. But I was on a real sexual high. Every time I looked at Justin, a shiver went right through me. Peter fell asleep in the taxi. Justin and I didn't say much, but we couldn't stop looking at each other and smiling. I knew then that we'd take it further, but I didn't think it would be that night.

The taxi pulled up and I got Peter out. Justin said, 'Do you want a hand?' I knew what he meant: did I want him to come in? I did. So he got out of the taxi and helped me get Peter into bed. Peter was absolutely dead to the world. I sensed something might happen, but I couldn't believe we'd do it in Peter's house, with him asleep in the next room.

I put on some music and offered Justin a coffee. We started messing around like a couple of kids, grabbing each other's coffee spoons. I put my spoon behind my back and Justin put both arms around me to grab it. We were nose to nose, and we stayed like that, staring at each other, for what felt like ages. It was the most sexually thrilling moment of my life. Were we going to go for it? Who was going to make the first move? Could we really be this naughty? Oh yes, we could. I put my arms around Justin and kissed him hard. He didn't hesitate, and kissed me back.

We couldn't get enough of each other. I remember touching him all over, kissing him everywhere. I'd wanted him for so long, and now we were actually doing what I'd fantasised about. I did wish Peter wasn't in the next room, because I had one eye on the door, but I guess it added to the thrill.

After two years with Peter, it was fantastic to be touched so passionately, and in so many new ways. With Peter, I always took the lead. Now Justin was in charge, and I loved it. He lifted me up onto the kitchen worktop, kissed me all down my front and gave me oral sex beside the kettle.

Justin was very, very good at it. He used his fingers and tongue at the same time, which felt incredible, and I came right there on Peter's kitchen worktop. I sat up, wrapped my legs around him and we had sex on it, with Justin standing up. It was fast, hard and very passionate, with just enough emotion to make sure I really let myself go. With a one-night stand, I'm always on guard, not knowing much about the person. But with Justin, I knew him, I knew he cared about me, so I wasn't embarrassed or self-conscious. I just didn't want Peter walking in the door . . .

Justin came quickly, but we carried on kissing and touching each other afterwards, as if coming wasn't enough for us. By now I'd lost track of time and I really didn't want Peter to catch us, so I climbed off the worktop, pulled down my dress, found my knickers on the floor and finished making the coffee, with Justin's arms around me from behind. We often hugged, so if Peter walked in on that, especially in his drunken state, I knew he wouldn't suspect. I hoped he wouldn't see it in my eyes.

We had a coffee, still touching and kissing. I told Justin I was going to split up with Peter, and he looked panic-stricken. I realised he thought I wanted us to become an item, which wasn't my plan at all, and I told him so. Maybe if we'd met first

– but he was Peter's best friend and there was no way either of us could do that to him. Justin agreed. He said he'd never slept with any of Peter's girlfriends, but when it came to me, he couldn't resist. I still get a kick out of that.

When Justin left, I got into bed beside Peter and fell asleep. I felt very guilty and I knew we'd split up. We had to. I ended it the following day, but I didn't say a word about what I'd done. Justin did call me to see if I was OK, and we still meet up every few weeks for a drink, a chat – and some very, very good sex. He's still dating a string of girls, but I get the best of both worlds – a good friend and great sex when I want it. Maybe if he grows up one day we'll make a go of it. Peter is now engaged to someone else, as Justin says, 'someone quieter and much more his type'. I'm just so relieved that Peter never found out that both his girlfriend and his best friend betrayed him. He doesn't deserve that.

Helen, 27

She confesses (girl–girl)

I made love to my boyfriend's sister

When Ally gave her the come-on, Sara couldn't resist . . .

Let's face it: my boyfriend Stephen is pretty. A perfect, chiselled nose, big brown eyes behind long dark lashes . . . you know the type. Could be a model. Probably should be. Stick Stephen's face on anything from light-bulbs to Levi's and I swear we'd be queuing up. He is just irresistible. The trouble is, so is his sister. I couldn't say no. To either of them.

I met Stephen through my ex, Mark. At first, we had the

classic flirty friendship. The one you always have with your boyfriend's best mate. But it went further. Stephen confided he loved me. I was flattered. Tempted, even. But Mark and I were an item, totally besotted with each other. Or so I thought.

Then Mark dumped me. Not even to my face. He got one of his mates to tell me. On the phone. Six hot, horny, love-crazy months wiped out. I can't even remember the pathetic story. Something like, 'Mark needs some personal space,' or some crap like that. Guess who picked up the pieces? Stephen was my shoulder to sob on, my best friend. The one who finally persuaded me to go out after two weeks in hibernation.

We went to a party. Mark was going to be there. I needed to – had to – talk to him. Ask the bastard 'WHY?' That was the only way I could forget about it and move on. Or, if I'm honest, see if we could get back together.

It was a disaster. Our 'chat' lasted two minutes. Mark said, 'I can't love you, never did, never could and never can.' That told me. But what the hell did it mean? (I found out later that he'd decided he was gay.) I was left on the sofa, depressed, upset, totally ugly and unlovable.

Maybe that's why it happened. Maybe I had to prove I was still attractive. Maybe I was sick of being hurt by men. Maybe I wanted to sleep with Stephen but I wasn't ready for the emotional commitment. I loved him, fancied him, but it was too soon to think of a new relationship. So I ended up in bed with his sister.

I'd seen Ally around a few times. She was gorgeous. Just like Stephen, only prettier, more elegant. Two years younger. I knew she was bisexual, but I hadn't felt sexually attracted to her until that night.

Ally was sitting on the floor beside me. The party was crowded, smoky and loud. I was desperate to feel wanted. Then I looked at her soft, dark hair caressing her bare shoulders and I wanted to touch it. So I did.

I thought Ally would brush my hand away or move out of

reach, but she didn't. She turned and smiled at me. She looked so much like Stephen, only gentler, softer. I felt safe. I knew she wouldn't hurt me.

My fingers moved to caress her face. Then I slid down onto the floor beside her. Ally stroked my face too. It was the most incredible, intense feeling – so sexual. I was very wet by now, and I wanted more than stroking. I wanted sex. We kissed gently at first, then harder. I'd never kissed a woman before. This was more than just kissing Ally, though. I was kissing Stephen too.

We kissed for ages. Then I put my hands inside her top and stroked her breasts. As I touched her nipples, she moaned and dropped her fingers between my legs, rubbing my clitoris through my trousers. We masturbated each other through our clothes for almost an hour. I was very close to orgasm and, as I ran my finger over her pants, I knew she was too. We had to finish this in private.

When we got upstairs, reality hit her. Ally said we had to talk. She knew how much her brother loved me. And she had a boyfriend, too. Having sex with me was hurting people she loved. There was no future – we had to stop.

I was so confused and so horny that all I wanted to do was come in Ally's arms. But I understood why she couldn't. So I went home from the party alone, even more lonely and upset than when I got there. As I sobered up, I couldn't believe what I'd done. I wanted Stephen but I was too afraid, so I went for Ally instead. Stephen must have seen us. How could we ever have a relationship now I'd done that with his sister?

When I saw Stephen, I felt embarrassed. He was as lovely as ever. We didn't mention Ally at first, then he said, 'You could have been a bit more subtle last night.' The look in his eyes told me how much I'd hurt him. I knew then how much I loved him. We had to work things out.

The sexual tension between us built up and up from that day.

Having been with Ally simply heightened it. There was a real barrier between us now that had to be broken. But it had to happen. Then one night, he kissed me. Sex was so intense, yet slow and sensual, that when I orgasmed I felt like I was floating off the bed. This time I was sleeping with the 'real thing'. It was absolutely fantastic.

We've been together for three years now. Our sex life is hot, but deep and caring too. He's the most fulfilling lover I've ever known. Ally and I are friends. We don't mention what happened, and neither do Stephen's mates – not in my earshot, anyway. Stephen and I do sometimes laugh about 'the Ally thing'. It's weird that they both fancied me. He's never asked any questions about it, but I think he knows the score. If we do get married one day, I just hope the best man's speech doesn't allude to it.

Sara, 27

She confesses (boy–girl)

My sex romp with his dad

Julie thought Rob was the man of her dreams – until she had dinner with his father . . .

This wasn't lust at first sight. Sure, I thought Rob's dad was good-looking, but older men aren't my style. Not *that* much older, anyway. Peter was in his early fifties, with grey-blond hair and a face that reminded me of Michael Douglas. Why would I be interested when I had the younger version? Rob was plenty for me to handle. Then I had dinner with Peter, just the two of us. By coffee time I was giving him the best blow-job of his life.

The irony is that Rob suggested it. Not the blow-job, you understand – the dinner. He was going away to a conference in Brussels for three days. 'Dad thought you were coming with me and asked if he could stay in our flat on Saturday night if it was empty. He's going to a show in the afternoon.'

I knew where this was heading. Rob never, ever said 'no' to his father. No one ever did. 'He can stay in the spare room,' Rob went on. 'It's only Dad. Mum's on a bridge weekend.' Then, seeing the expression on my face, he added, 'Why don't you two go out for dinner? My treat. Anywhere you like. It's only for one night . . .'

I've got to admit, it was tempting. I could impress my potential father-in-law, get in Rob's good books and enjoy a free dinner. There was also the chance to find out a few juicy titbits about Rob. Peter was a real raconteur and, I suspected, a lot more fun without Rob's mum around. She was starchy, and only interested if you played bridge or prefaced your name with 'Lady'. So I agreed. I didn't think for a moment I'd get first-class sex thrown in too.

Rob left early on Friday morning – but not before we'd had a pretty full-on sex session. 'Just so you don't forget me by Sunday,' he grinned. I didn't want him to forget me either, so when he was close to orgasm inside me, I slid down and sucked until he came. Oral sex was his favourite. He'd confessed it once, but he didn't need to. Hearing him gasp and groan as I ran my tongue over the head of his penis told me that this was what he liked best. By Sunday I hadn't forgotten him – and I'd found out what his father liked best, too.

Friday night turned into a heavy girls' night out, and when Peter arrived at Saturday lunchtime, I was still fast asleep in bed. So much for impressing him. I staggered to the door, headache pounding, reeking of stale wine, convinced it was 7 a.m. and that I'd be greeted by the postman.

Peter apologised endlessly for waking me up, and put his overnight bag in the spare room while I made us both a coffee. The sexual vibe was there even then, if I'm honest. Maybe it was seeing him without Rob. When Rob was around, Peter automatically went into 'dad' mode, confident and in charge. But alone in the flat, we were just a man and a woman. I looked at him in a whole new light. We always saw Peter at his place in the country, which was all long walks and formal dinners. This was my turf and much more casual. Peter was more humble and eager to please. But I still didn't think anything would ever come of it.

I booked dinner at the Waldorf, because I knew he'd been there with Rob. But by late afternoon, my hangover was still triggering waves of nausea, and I couldn't face the formality of it. When Peter got back, I asked if he'd like me to cook instead. He said he'd be delighted.

Maybe I sensed what was coming. Maybe he did, too. Maybe that's why I didn't want to go out. If so, I wasn't consciously aware of it. I kept the atmosphere casual with pasta, a simple carbonara sauce, and lots of red wine. Sade on the stereo. The conversation – and the wine – flowed like a dream. Peter was so much like Rob, but more experienced, wiser, calmer and, in the candlelight, he was looking more attractive than Rob by the second.

He had vanilla ice-cream with his coffee; I had chocolate. He wanted to try mine, so we fed each other Häagen-Dazs. Trust me, it isn't corny when you actually do it. I moved round to sit next to him. The sexual attraction between us was so intense that I felt myself getting wet every time he put the spoon in my mouth. The fact he was Rob's dad was giving me a sexual thrill that I'd never felt before.

The ice-cream was melting rapidly and, as I leaned towards him with my spoon, some of it dripped on his lap. Without thinking, I grabbed a napkin and dabbed at it. That's when I felt his erection. He groaned as my fingers pressed on his penis. I looked up into his eyes and saw excitement, guilt, disbelief, even panic. He was wondering what the hell I was going to do or say. So was I. But I unzipped his fly, said, 'I think I know what you need,' bent forwards and gave him oral sex.

Peter came quickly, but I didn't care. I knew we were going to be making love all night. I moved over to the sofa, opened my legs and he buried his face between them, licking and sucking my clitoris until I came. He was hard again, so he climbed on top and went inside me. That was the weirdest part, because he felt exactly like Rob. I'd been too turned on to notice it before, but his penis was pretty much the same shape and thickness as Rob's. It didn't stop me.

That night, I reached sexual highs I'd never experienced before. We made love four or five times, and in between we touched and kissed each other, totally unable to stop. He was fantastic in bed, but I know the biggest kick was the fact he was Rob's dad. I can't even blame the drink, because we carried on way past the time I'd sobered up.

It was the telephone that woke me. I'd finally fallen asleep upside-down in bed, in Peter's arms. Rob sounded as chirpy as ever. 'Didn't wake you up, did I? How's Dad?'

What could I say? I stammered 'still in bed' and promised to ring him back when I woke up properly. The guilt kicked in for both of us. Peter got straight out of bed, pulled on his trousers, apologised and said he hadn't meant to do it. The atmosphere was pretty tense. I didn't regret what I'd done – how could I ever regret such amazing sex? But I was worried about what it would do to my relationship with Rob.

I figured the best way to handle things was to calm Peter down. I told him it was cool, just 'one of those things'. We need never mention it again. I didn't feel very calm, but I did a pretty good impression of someone who was taking it all in their stride. We had a coffee, and Peter said it was the best blow-job he'd ever had. Inside, I was freaking out. That's exactly what Rob said to me when we first made love.

When Peter left, we parted as friends. There was no way either of us could cope emotionally with having sex again. I spent the rest of the day feeling excited as I relived it in my mind, and terrified that Rob would know something was up.

He didn't, of course. The fresh sheets, fresh flowers, tidy flat and talking about how much I'd missed him saw to that. When we made love that night, I couldn't get images of Peter out of my head. This warm, loving sex was satisfying, but it didn't blow my mind the way sex with Peter had.

I'm still with Rob, but I've spent the last few months avoiding all his family parties. It's caused tension between us. Rob doesn't understand why I don't want to go. I know I'll have to see Peter some day. I just hope no one sees what's in our eyes when we look at each other.

Julie, 28

9
The Show Must Go On

Lights, camera, action! In our final selection, raunchy *Cosmo* readers give the performances of their lives – from the guy who acts out his fantasy as Batman to the couple whose serious love scene on stage becomes a live sex show. A drama queen camps it up to win a girl's trust, and our artist's model steals the show with her erotic poses . . .

There's stage fright, too, for the couple who find out their sex romp is caught on CCTV, and the girl who gives her boyfriend a private sex show – and finds an uninvited guest in the audience. Encore!

She confesses (boy–girl)

I had sex in front of 250 people

Anna treated the theatre audience to a real live sex scene . . .

Believe me, it gets worse. Not only did I have sex in the middle of a very serious play, in front of a sell-out crowd, but my parents and younger sister were in the audience. To this day, they have no idea they were watching the 'real thing'. At least, I hope they don't . . .

I couldn't believe my luck when I landed a leading role in the production. On stage, my relationship with the leading man was quite stormy, and I knew I'd have to kiss him, so when I arrived for the first script read-through, I was praying he was gorgeous.

Mark was better than gorgeous. I'd never fancied anyone so much in my life. Short dark hair, cute bum, fabulous smile – for a second, I thought he was too good-looking to be straight. Then we caught each other's eye, and I knew he wasn't gay. There was a sexual spark between us from that moment on, which worked brilliantly off stage and on – and the show sold out for its entire week-long run.

I realised early on that I didn't want a relationship with Mark – he was too much of a flirt. Just sex was fine by me. The sexual tension between us built up over the weeks of rehearsals. At the end of the final scene, we had to fall backwards onto the bed and pretend to make love as the bed slowly revolved away from the audience, marking the end of the play. Each time we did, it felt more passionate and real. I often fantasised about it afterwards. Something had to happen. I thought we'd get it on at the after-show party on the last night. I didn't think it would happen on stage in front of an audience . . .

Everyone was pretty fired up on the last day. We'd had a great run, the show was a huge success and we were running on excitement and adrenaline. We performed a matinée in the afternoon, and the final show was that evening. My parents and sixteen-year-old sister had travelled up from London to watch it. Emotions were running high, too – we'd all enjoyed working together and this was our last day as a team.

When we reached our final scene that evening, I felt very emotional – this could be the last time I ever got to kiss Mark. I guess he felt the same way, because this time the kiss was totally real. Neither of us were acting. We kissed for much longer than usual – God knows what the rest of the cast and crew were thinking. The thought of all those people in the audience watching – and not realising this was real – turned me on, and I felt myself getting wet. I felt powerful, too – we were ending the play our way!

We fell backwards onto the bed and pulled the duvet over us.

Normally, Mark climbed on top and we rolled around, pretending to make love, as the lights dimmed, the bed revolved and the final curtain fell. But this time, I felt Mark's huge erection pressing through his trousers. I was so wet by now that I just wanted to feel him inside me. The lights began to dim. I reached down, unzipped his trousers and pulled out his penis. He groaned, just loud enough for me to hear.

The bed hadn't started revolving, so I knew we had a minute, maybe two at most. Luckily I was wearing a short skirt, so I just pulled my knickers to one side and guided his penis inside me, masturbating myself with my finger.

The bed began to move. Mark thrust inside me faster and faster. I thought of all the people watching us, but I was so turned on that it just made me hornier. I came hard – but quietly. Mark came seconds later, with a slightly too loud grunt. The lights went out completely, the curtain fell and the audience burst into applause. Mark and I burst out laughing. We just had time to adjust our clothes before the bed came to a halt. The rest of the cast ran over to congratulate us on our 'best love scene yet'. A few of them winked. I'm sure they thought we'd had a bit of a grope – but no one realised we'd managed full sex!

We went straight back on stage to take our bow, and received several encores – though we didn't treat everyone to a repeat performance! I was on such a high from the show – and the sex – that I didn't feel embarrassed or worried about what I'd done. Mark and I just grinned at each other. It was only when I met Mum and Dad straight afterwards that I thought, 'Oh my God. How could I do that? What if they noticed? What if everyone noticed?' But I could tell my parents, thought it was just very good acting.

Mum and Dad took me out for dinner, as we'd arranged, and I went back to the theatre afterwards for the after-show party. Mark didn't turn up. Apparently he left straight after the show. Maybe he doesn't like goodbyes; maybe he was embarrassed;

maybe he thought I'd want a relationship; maybe he wasn't used to girls taking the initiative like that. I'll never know. I hope he doesn't regret it. I certainly don't – and I still get a kick when I think of the audience not knowing what they had really watched!

Anna, 26

He confesses (boy–girl)

I was a superhero for a night

Ian didn't usually confess his ultimate fantasy, and was convinced he'd never live it out. Then he met Karen . . .

Call it a boy thing, if you like. God knows what a shrink would make of it, but I've always wanted to be a superhero. I had three older brothers, so I was always playing catch-up. I was too far down the pecking order to even play Robin. Same story at work – I'm just one of the team, nothing special. Then Michelle Pfeiffer played Catwoman in one of the Batman films. Gorgeous. I was hooked. Having sex with Catwoman – while dressed as Batman – became my secret fantasy. I had to do it. But how?

Most girls laughed at my Batman videos. I played it down, saying they were for my nine-year-old nephew. But I knew there was no way they'd be up for acting out my fantasy. Then I met Karen. She was very pretty and quieter than my usual type. She worked at my firm. We were friends at first. Then we ended up in bed after a drunken Christmas party.

When I woke up, I thought I'd get lumbered. Sorry to be blunt, but I was worried she was playing hunt-a-husband. But she left straight after breakfast. She didn't expect me to spend the day with her. I liked that. So I called her. We dated. The sex was OK, but she was pretty shy in bed too. Batman didn't stand a chance.

Then she noticed my Batman videos. She said they were great, and that Michelle Pfeiffer looked 'gorgeous'. I couldn't believe my luck. So we watched one. I don't know why, but I confessed my fantasy. Maybe I felt safe with Karen. Maybe it was because I didn't think I stood a chance of it coming true with her.

Karen didn't laugh, thank God. That was always my biggest fear. She listened. Afterwards, we had sex. She was hotter, more passionate than usual. I felt closer to her, too. But we didn't mention Batman again. I thought she'd forgotten about it. She hadn't, though.

On my birthday, Karen booked us a night at a top London hotel. I was impressed. We had dinner in Soho and wandered back to our room overlooking the London Eye. Karen broke straight into the mini-bar. She'd been knocking it back all night. I was about to find out why.

There was a parcel on the bed with a massive bow on it. Karen said, 'Aren't you going to open your birthday present?' I had no idea what it was. I ripped open the packaging and a full-size Batman outfit fell onto the bed. I was so shocked that I didn't say anything. Karen took the lead, for the first time ever. She put out most of the lights and told me to put Batman on while she got changed in the bathroom.

It was lucky I'd had a lot to drink. The outfit was incredible – padded chest, cape, mask – the works. But I felt a right prat standing there in it. I half expected Jeremy Beadle to burst out of a cupboard. It was all-in-one, so I couldn't do the back up, either. I lay down on the bed and prayed she was changing into Catwoman. The idea turned me on. There was no hiding my erection in this outfit.

When Karen came out of the bathroom, I gasped. She was

wearing a skin-tight PVC catsuit with a tail, cat mask and whip. I was already hard but when I saw her, I almost came. She walked round the bed, cat-like, in full character, saying, 'I've got you now, Batman. You have to do exactly what I tell you.' Then she climbed on top of me, rubbing herself against my penis. I don't know how I stopped myself climaxing.

It was the best sex I've ever had. Not even a fantasy can touch it. It sounds corny, but we called each other 'Batman' and 'Catwoman'. What a turn-on. We were both well into it. For those two hours, I was Batman. Neither of us wanted to take the outfits off, so we touched each other all over, kissing and rubbing each other through them until we couldn't stand it any longer. Then we ripped them off and had full, explosive sex – still wearing our masks. I wanted her to come first, so I pulled out and brought her to orgasm with my tongue. When I finally came inside her, it was the most intense, passionate orgasm I've ever had.

Afterwards, we fell asleep. It was so good that neither of us wanted to do it again and spoil the memory. Next morning, sober, we were embarrassed. There's no getting away from it. We hadn't shut the curtains so the sunlight woke us up at 5 a.m. The Batman and Catwoman outfits – and all my clothes – were strewn around the floor. I said, 'I hope you didn't hire them or you'll lose the deposit.' That broke the ice.

Karen and I are still together. What she did was more than fulfil a fantasy. She brought us closer. Once you've shared a night like that, your whole relationship moves up a gear. Sex between us now is incredible, the best. We still wear the outfits sometimes, but nothing will ever touch that night. It's the best birthday present I've ever had.

Ian, 30

She confesses (boy–girl–boy)

I stripped for my man, and his brother watched

When Sarah decided to strip for her boyfriend, she thought it would be for his eyes only . . .

My boyfriend David had a body to die for. The way his dark hair flopped over his sparky blue eyes made me want to rip his suit off and lick him all over. But I didn't. And I wasn't sure why not. After all, I'd done that to my ex and he wasn't anywhere near as horny.

Maybe that was the problem. David was cool and confident. Not arrogant, but the sort of guy who walked round my flat with my tiny white hand-towel knotted round his firm, tanned middle, turning me on like crazy, and didn't give it a second thought. The sort of guy who took the lead in bed. We'd been together for three months and the sex was amazing. He was so good at teasing me to orgasm that I just went with it. With David, I came every time. That was a first for me.

But I longed to really let myself go. I fantasised about going down on him. Sucking until he was screaming for more. I think he sensed I was holding back, because one night after sex he whispered he'd love to see me masturbate. He wanted a 'sex show'. Just thinking about it turned me on so much that we had sex again. But I didn't think I'd ever have the confidence to do it. Not for him – I wouldn't be good enough.

Then he came to see me in my first musical. Don't worry, I'm not a real luvvy type. I just had a small part as a dancer. Before the show, I was so scared I thought I was going to throw up. Afterwards, I was so relieved that I downed loads of free champagne. David had brought his younger brother Liam to meet me. He was almost as good-looking as David, but only seventeen and very shy. David reckoned he was still a virgin.

So I guess I was pretty intimidating in a high-cut leotard, tiara, feather boa, stilettos and heavy make-up.

After the party, a group of us went back to David's flat. Liam made his excuses and went off to bed. I don't think it was his scene at all. We knocked back a few more bottles of champagne. By the time the others crashed out in the room next door, I was very drunk and on a real high from the show. I don't know what came over me. Maybe it was my costume, too. I thought, 'If David wants a sex show, let's give him one.'

I unzipped his trousers and sucked him hard. David moaned with pleasure. I was really into it. I'm sure it was the best blow-job I've ever given. There was nothing to hold me back. David whispered we should carry on in the bedroom – he was worried our friends might come back in. I didn't care, but when David said it twice I knew it was really bothering him.

I stood up and pushed him through the bedroom door. Being in charge of David was my fantasy. Now it was coming true, and it felt even better than I'd dreamed. I shoved him onto the bed and sexily took off my feather boa. The light was dim, but I could see David's face. 'I'm going to tie you up,' I told him. I lifted his arms over his head and tied them to his iron bedpost. When he pretended to struggle, I snapped, 'Be quiet' like some kind of amateur dominatrix. I'd never done anything like this before, but I loved it. Judging by the size of his erection, David was seriously turned on. I sucked him a bit more, then I stood up and started to strip.

I slid my leotard down to my waist and leaned forward so he could see my breasts. David hadn't touched me yet and I was very horny, so I licked and massaged them. He told me I was driving him wild and that he was 'going to explode' unless I untied him so he could masturbate. That got me going even more. I felt confident and proud of myself for doing it. As I touched myself, I described it too – 'licking my erect nipples', 'sliding my hand down to my wet clitoris'. David was squirming around on the bed in a frenzy, trying to rub his penis on the duvet.

I pulled my leotard off and climbed onto David's chest of drawers. He'd asked for a sex show and I was going to give him one. I sat on the top, leaned back, opened my legs and masturbated until I came, talking dirty and practically screaming when I orgasmed. Then I climbed on top of David, and he came the moment he was inside me.

David told me I'd been sexy on stage, but this was something else. We lay there exhausted for a few minutes, then we had sex again. By the time we'd finished, I'd sobered up a lot, but we'd had such a good time that I didn't regret it or feel embarrassed at all, though I was surprised I'd done it. Proud, too. I was sure our sex life would be even better from now on.

During our first sex session, I'd vaguely noticed David's clock radio come on. But as we lay there a couple of hours later, trying to get to sleep, the radio was keeping me awake. David said to leave it, but I couldn't. So I climbed out of bed, feeling a bit sore and sober, and staggered across the room. That's when I saw him. Liam. Lying on the bedroom floor in a sleeping-bag, wide awake.

Our eyes met. Locked, more like. Liam's eyes were full of shock and embarrassment. I knew he must have seen – and heard – the whole thing. He'd put the radio on to try to drown us out. My entire sex show raced through my mind like a video on fast forward. My God – he'd seen me do that. And say that. And come on the cabinet. I was so embarrassed and ashamed that I wished it had never happened.

Liam coughed quietly and looked away. I turned off the radio and went back to bed. David launched into another, 'I loved it when you went down on me.' I hissed at him to be quiet and whispered that Liam was lying awake on the floor. David went completely silent.

We lay there almost terrified to move. At least Liam looked

like he'd tried to sleep through it. I was sure he hadn't got a kick out of my show (though I guessed he might do at a later date, which was mortifying).

Eventually, I fell asleep. When I woke up, it was one of those classic mornings when it all comes back to you slowly. I didn't feel too bad about what I'd done, though I realised that, being so drunk, my strip show must have been pretty wobbly and uncoordinated. But I was worried that David might think badly of me. And the thought of Liam seeing and hearing our sex session was horrendous. He probably thought David had paired up with some sex-mad dominatrix.

I went for some water and found Liam had moved his sleeping-bag into the living room. David was really jolly and jokey about it all. He asked me if that was the sort of thing I always did on a Friday night. That upset me a bit (because it wasn't) and I told him so. David apologised, hugged me and said he loved it. When Liam got up, we all had a cup of tea and chatted about work. I could hardly look him in the eye. No one mentioned what had happened.

It's been two years now. David and I are still together. Our sex life is definitely more spicy – I really let go. Liam has never mentioned it or even vaguely alluded to it, even when drunk. But I still cringe when I think about my drunken sex show. When I strip for David, I always make sure now that we're definitely alone.

Sarah, 27

He confesses (boy–girl)

I pretended to be gay – and then seduced her

Daniel knew Lisa adored gay guys, so he camped it up to win her trust . . .

Everyone fancied Lisa. Even our hard-hearted, no-nonsense MD melted when Lisa turned on the charm. Blonde, bubbly and bloody good at her sales job, every single guy in my office had asked her out at least once – and even a few of the married ones had tried their luck. But Lisa always said no. Then I played my trump card, camping it up until I'd give Julian Clary a run for his money. Without the make-up, of course. But my plan worked, and I succeeded in getting Lisa into bed, even if it was for one night only.

God, what I did sounds unforgivable – and it was. I'm not proud of myself. My one saving grace is that Lisa still doesn't know it was a trick. She thinks I had a sexual identity crisis and decided I was bi. She even offered me her shoulder to cry on while I sorted myself out. I didn't have the heart to tell her it was a dirty scam to get her into bed.

Lisa worked in the same sales firm as me, but not in our office. Word was that she had boyfriends outside work, nothing serious, and plenty of male friends who often met her after work for a drink. Several of them were gay. I'd seen her in the pub with them, and they were obviously very close. We were all having a drink one night when our office secretary caught me staring hopefully across the bar at Lisa, and piped up, 'You haven't got a hope, Dan. Unless you pretend to be gay.'

My mate Steve grinned and said, 'Now, there's a thought.' I laughed it off, but it put the idea in my head. At work, I asked Steve if he thought it was worth a shot. Steve's pretty homophobic, so his advice was, 'Not unless you want the whole place to think you're a bloody poof.' That didn't bother me at all. I didn't care what people thought, and I'd only need to camp it up around Lisa, anyway. But I did confide in Steve so at least he knew what was going on.

I'm always smartly dressed for work, but I started using aftershave and making sure I was immaculate every day, even when I had a hangover. I had to put up with a load of 'bloody hell, Dan, what's that niff?' and 'he's got the Lynx effect' comments from the lads – for the record, it was CK One – but what the hell. Bumping into Lisa by the photocopier or coffee machine was simple. I even timed it so I could chat to her in the sandwich queue. Being camp made it easy for me to talk to her. She'd never even noticed me before, and I hadn't had the confidence to chat her up.

I've met enough gay men to know that they're often real heart-on-your-sleeve jobs, much more open and honest than the rest of us. I practised the mannerisms and voice at home. I'm still amazed at how easy it was. Steve'll kill me for saying this, but I reckon us guys repress all that stuff and try to be macho without even realising it.

Lying was harder. Soon, Lisa was looking out for me at work to say 'hi' to, and we started having lunch. Lisa never asked if I was gay, but I talked openly to her about my male partners and said I wasn't 'out' at work. I had to invent an entire sexual history for myself. Working in sales, I'm used to stretching the truth, but this was made up from scratch. The only way I could do it was to pretend all my ex-girlfriends were men. I'd been with my previous girlfriend, Jo – who became Joe – for three years before she dumped me. Remembering to say 'he' not 'she' was a complete nightmare, and I did slip up a couple of times, but I covered it up by being excessively camp and calling Joe a 'bitch'.

Then came a bombshell. Lisa asked if I'd like to meet some of her gay friends. She thought I might fancy some of them. I panicked. They'd know I was a fraud – they'd see it in my eyes. I told her I wasn't ready for a relationship, or new friends, just yet. Lisa looked surprised but accepted it. The irony is that when I talked to Lisa, I was honest about my feelings – how hurt I'd been by Jo, about growing up with Mum and Dad – I just lied about my sexuality. I began to wish I'd chatted her up on the level. Lisa told me all kinds of stuff about herself because she trusted me. One night, she confessed that she was wary of getting to know straight men because they always made a play for her. I did feel a bit of a bastard, but I couldn't back off now.

After two months of it, Lisa and I had become close. We'd been to the cinema, had lunch, got drunk in the pub – staying 'gay' and not flirting was hard that night – and I was sexually frustrated beyond belief. I masturbated while fantasising about her all the time, but I wanted the real thing. So I invited her to my place for dinner.

The flat was a pigsty, but by the time I'd finished, it would do any queen proud. Flowers in vases, towels on the racks. I even cleaned the loo. She looked stunning in a pink dress and said she'd worn pink especially for me. If only she knew the truth . . .

I topped up Lisa's glass far too often and she got very drunk. By dessert, I'd dropped the mannerisms and was looking lustfully across the table at her. She picked up the vibe and looked back at me, puzzled. Then she banged down her glass and said suddenly, 'Why are all the guys I really like gay? If you were straight, I'd really fancy you.'

It was now or never. I took her hand across the table and gently kissed it. Then I moved around next to her and kissed her all the way up her arm to her shoulder. She said, 'That feels really nice.' I told her she was gorgeous, sat down beside her and kissed her on the lips.

I get hard just thinking about it. She didn't say a word, she just went with the flow. Two months' worth of sexual frustration meant I was ready for some fast, hard sex, but I held back. I didn't want to scare her off now. We kissed for ages, as if neither of us wanted to make the first move to take it further. Then I slid my hand between her legs. She eased them apart, saying, 'Are you sure this is what you want?' Too bloody right it was.

I masturbated her slowly at first, then faster, and brought her to orgasm on the chair. She still hadn't touched me, and I was so hard I slipped my other hand inside my trousers to masturbate. Lisa whispered, 'Do you want to make love?' She led me through into the bedroom, lay me down on the bed and climbed on top of me. As we made love gently, she said, 'Is this your first time with a woman?' I was too far gone to lie. Thank God I said no, because after that the sex went from being gentle to fast, hard and with lots of swearing. We brought each other to orgasm together with oral sex, and when I came, it was totally explosive.

I was up for a repeat performance, but when Lisa woke up a couple of hours later, she was very upset and apologised for having sex with me. I told her I was absolutely fine – that was the understatement of the year – but she insisted that she'd got drunk and started it. I couldn't tell her the truth – I knew her well enough to know she'd never forgive me, so I said that maybe I'd just found out I was bi. When I asked her to stay the night, Lisa said she wanted to go home – but if I needed to talk, she'd be there for me. She apologised again and said, 'You're going to have some thinking to do.'

Lisa cooled off our friendship after that night. I missed her. I even called and told her I'd like to date her, but Lisa said it would be 'too complicated'. Steve thought I was the luckiest bloke on earth to get a night with Lisa, and in a way, I was. But I'll never know just how many nights I would have got if I'd played it straight.

Daniel, 28

She confesses (boys–girl)

My surprise sex show for fifteen men

When Susannah decided to earn some extra cash as an artists'
model, she didn't realise just how much she'd enjoy it . . .

Drama school was everything I'd dreamed of, but it left me
virtually penniless. So I turned to modelling. I enjoyed it, too –
so much that, in my last session, I put on a farewell sex show.
It drove me wild, and the audience was pretty impressed, too.

I met Philip on a night when my friend Joanne, a rich girl
from college, stood me up. She'd invited me to a members-only
club her dad belonged to, all expenses paid. It was pretty flash
and full of older men – the kind of place I'd normally avoid like
the plague. I checked my watch. It was 8 p.m. We'd definitely
agreed on 7.45 p.m. I spent a ghastly hour standing at the bar,
looking and feeling like the club prostitute. Joanne wasn't even
answering her mobile. I'd just plotted my revenge by telling the
course creep that she really fancied him, when a kind-looking
guy in his late fifties walked over.

Come on, I know what you're thinking, but it wasn't like
that. To this day – and I've got to know him well – I still think
he'd noticed I was anxious and came over to see if I was OK.
Of course, I didn't think that at first, and when he offered me a
drink, I refused. But we got chatting and I stayed in the bar all
night. Joanne didn't show up, but I didn't care. Philip was far
more interesting to talk to.

Philip was – and still is – an artist and sculptor. His work is
incredible, full of energy and life. Despite the age gap, we were
on the same wavelength. I'd never met anyone like him, so
charming and 'old school'. He wasn't good-looking, but there
was something erotic about him. Maybe it was the way he
talked about art. He was immaculately dressed, with short grey

hair and an open and caring manner I'd only ever encountered in gay men. I like that.

When I left the club – completely plastered – he put me in a cab and paid the driver to take me home. That felt good, really good. There was something sexual between us, but I didn't want to have sex with him, or even let him touch me. I didn't know what it was.

We met the next day at his studio. His nudes were incredible – from graphic charcoal drawings to huge, colourful portraits. Then I remembered the pictures in Madonna's *Sex* book of her being touched by an older man. I wanted to model for him. I wanted him to look at my body the way he'd studied those girls, to admire it, to adore it, to need it – but not be able to have it. This wasn't a tease, it was just the relationship between an artist and a model. That feeling of power would drive me wild.

Philip was surprised but thrilled when I offered to model for him. He explained that sessions last ninety minutes, and I'd get paid £40. I agreed, so he arranged a platform under the window in his studio and covered it with a velvet cloth. I was nervous when I took my clothes off, but Philip was professional and put me at ease. He arranged me in a pose and was so flattering to my body shape that I lapped up the attention. The sun streamed in through the window, warming me and the velvet. Being looked at and admired naked gave me such an incredible feeling of power. I felt very turned on. If someone had told me I'd get off on nude modelling for an old man I hardly knew, I'd have laughed in their face. But here I was, doing just that, getting hornier by the second.

I shifted about on the velvet, trying to squeeze my clitoris. Philip reminded me to keep still. That turned me on even more. I was literally throbbing between the legs. When I looked across at Philip, his erection was bulging in his trousers. Knowing he was getting sexual pleasure from my body – and couldn't touch it – almost made me orgasm on the spot. I didn't feel threatened, as I trusted Philip.

After ninety minutes, Philip closed his sketch-book. I got dressed and he showed me the drawings. Maybe I'm biased, but I could feel the sexual energy in them. He knew I was turned on, too. I was sure of it. We arranged a second session, and when I got home I masturbated the moment I was in the front door. Literally. I dropped my bag on the hall floor, leaned against the wall, pulled down my jeans and masturbated roughly. I came within a minute.

I didn't tell my boyfriend about the modelling, but he noticed I found it easier to orgasm. All I had to do was fantasise about modelling, remember those feelings, and I'd come.

It was my suggestion to pose for the drawing class Philip took. Modelling for him alone was losing its sexual appeal, and the idea of posing for a group was too much to resist. I fantasised about it. He was reluctant at first, saying he didn't want to share me. But they were always short of models, and I persuaded him. Maybe it's the actress in me, but I desperately wanted an audience, a proper audience.

The session was held at a different studio. By the time I arrived, I wished I hadn't gone at all. It was colder, more formal. I downed a couple of glasses of wine. Philip noticed my nerves and said he'd take me home at any point if I didn't like it. I undressed and climbed onto the podium. Surprisingly, there were no women at all. There were about fifteen men with sketch-books and boards. Most were around Philip's age but some were younger. I scanned their faces to make sure I didn't know any of them. For my fantasy to work, they all had to be anonymous.

At first I didn't have that feeling of power – I felt vulnerable and ridiculous. But I wanted to take control of the situation – this was my one chance to live out my fantasy. After half an hour, we had a break, and I downed a couple more glasses of wine. When we started again, I struck an erotic pose and began to touch myself – subtly at first, then harder and faster.

Maybe it was the wine kicking in. Maybe I couldn't pass up the opportunity. Maybe it was being at stage school and having the chance to put on the sex show of a lifetime. Whatever made me do it, once I'd started, I couldn't stop. Someone in the room giggled appreciatively. Knowing those men were watching me, wanting me, drawing me, blew my mind. I held my pose but moved my hands around my inner thighs and clitoris. I orgasmed quickly – the thrill was too much! Closing my eyes for a second, my whole body shuddered. I felt so confident, so adored – like a goddess, being worshipped. It was as if everyone was there simply for my pleasure.

Afterwards, I didn't feel in any way embarrassed or ashamed – I'd lived out my fantasy and it was perfect. They'd even paid me £60 to do it.

I finished the session with less erotic poses, sitting with my body curled over my knees. No one said a word about my other poses, but their drawings were incredibly erotic – it was a turn-on just looking at myself. Philip planned to submit his to an erotic magazine. I still wonder whether they were published.

I continued to model for Philip, but purely for the money, until I left college. I touched myself sometimes but we never went beyond those limits – keeping a distance was the whole point. I didn't pose for the group again and I'd never tell my boyfriend. I might confess it as my fantasy, but I'll never admit I've acted it out.

Susannah, 29

She confesses (girl–girl)

My boyfriend caught me with a prostitute

Anne paid to make her dreams come true. She didn't plan on fulfilling Steve's fantasy too . . .

I'd fumbled around with girls before. You know, kissing and stroking, like you do when you're eleven and too young to date. By sixteen, I was well into sex with my boyfriend, and by 23, I'd been out with loads of guys and met Steve. But I couldn't help wondering what sex would be like with a woman. Just as a one-off. Just so I *knew*. That's why I paid to find out. I didn't think I'd get found out.

Steve and I worked together. I fancied him from the moment I saw him. He was very tall – six foot four – with reddish-blond hair, pale blue eyes and a shy, cute smile. 'Shy' was invented for him. How anyone that good-looking could be so shy was beyond me. But I sensed if I could get past that, we'd be in business.

He'd never make the first move, I was sure of it. So I did. I offered him a lift home and invited him in for coffee. That's all we had – coffee. It took two weeks to seduce him into bed. He was gentle at first, but once he warmed up, we had the best sex I'd ever experienced. Steve couldn't 'let go' in everyday life, but in bed with me, he was wild. Every time I saw him at work, all shy and quiet, I couldn't believe how different he was in the dark, in bed. Sex released him.

A year later, we moved in together. We even talked about marriage. But I was wary. My fantasies were more and more about women. I longed to find out what sex with a woman was like and every time I saw an attractive woman, my desire became almost uncontrollable. I wanted her to touch me, I *needed* her to. Was I bisexual? I didn't think so. This would be strictly a one-off, a kind of sex I'd never tried before. No strings, no commitment, and definitely no telling Steve. He'd freak out, I knew it, and feel completely betrayed, as if he wasn't good enough. Just goes to show how little you can know someone . . .

Gay bars were my first idea. But I didn't know the form. Did I just turn up on my own and look like an easy lay? Going with a friend meant I'd have to confide my fantasy. It sounded too complicated. There was also the risk that someone would get hurt emotionally. No, this had to be sex, just sex. For that, I needed a prostitute.

There were drawbacks. I wouldn't know what she looked like in advance. What if I didn't fancy her, or changed my mind about the whole idea? There'd be no flirting, no will she/won't she – just sex. But that's what I wanted, wasn't it? So I phoned in sick, waited until Steve had gone to work and pulled out his men's magazines. There were plenty of escort ads in the back.

The first escort agency was bloody rude. Told me their girls 'didn't do women'. So was the second. By the third, I was almost ready to give up. But the lady was very polite, almost mothering, and called me 'sweetheart'. I guess she twigged it was my first time. You'd think her manner would put me off, but it didn't – she gave me confidence. They had one girl in my area, Polly, who specialised in visiting 'ladies'. She was short, with long blonde hair, and charged £150 an hour. 'Guaranteed pleasure.' Did that mean guaranteed orgasm? Does she stay until you come? I was too embarrassed to ask.

I had no idea it would cost so much. But I wanted it, and I wanted it today. She could come at 4 p.m. That was fine – Steve usually got home around eight. I couldn't afford more than an hour, anyway.

At 10 a.m. it had sounded like a good idea. By 3.30 p.m. I was in a right state, wondering what the hell I'd done. I'd been down to the bank and withdrawn cash, had four showers, changed my clothes twice and almost had a panic attack. I almost had another one when the doorbell rang.

I shouldn't have worried. She was very pretty, very calm and totally in charge of the situation. My first thought was, 'Thank God I fancy her.'

Polly's 'driver' was waiting outside for the hour. Was that OK, or would I rather he parked around the corner? So polite. Either was fine by me – our London street was hardly full of twitching curtains. I didn't even know the neighbours' names.

I liked the fact she arrived with a driver. Somehow it made the whole experience feel less seedy, more professional. Polly came in and used her mobile to call the agency, confirm my address and her arrival time. Then I handed her the £150 and she asked if I'd like to go into the bedroom. We sat on the bed and she kissed me. Being touched by a woman felt amazing, so different for a man. Her touch was lighter, gentler, more confident. Polly stroked my breasts and worked down to my clitoris with her fingers and tongue. I copied her, and when I touched her clitoris and slipped my finger into her vagina, the intensity of the feeling that shot through me was unbelievable. She felt so different to me. I guess it's obvious that each guy will feel different, but it just hadn't occurred to me that every woman will, too.

Polly was a real pro. At first, each time I was close to orgasm, she pulled back. I lost track of time, but I guess she'd been there about 45 minutes when she gave me such amazing oral sex that I knew I was going to come. I opened my eyes to look down at her, which brought me even closer to orgasm, when I noticed Steve standing by the bedroom door, smiling. He wasn't masturbating, but the look on his face – and the massive bulge in his chinos – told me he was horny watching me. I came staring straight at him, which felt pretty weird. Polly worked her way back up my body, licking and kissing. When I opened my eyes, Steve had gone. I don't think she knew Steve had been watching but, being a professional, maybe she did and just carried on.

Polly got dressed, gave me her card, thanked me for booking her, and left. I put on my dressing-gown and went into the living room to face the music. Steve smiled and didn't say a word. He pulled me into the bedroom and we had the most passionate, frenzied, incredible sex I'd ever had. I talked dirty to him for the first time, telling him what I'd done with Polly, and what it felt like to lick another woman. When he came inside me, it was like an explosion.

Neither of us said a word about Polly until that night. Steve asked if she was a friend. I told the truth, and he was cool about it. I realised why when he confessed he'd come home from work early to check I was OK and found me fulfilling his favourite fantasy – to catch his girlfriend making love to another woman. He even said I could do it again, so long as he could watch. I wasn't up for that. Once was enough to satisfy my curiosity, convince me I'm heterosexual, and – by chance – give our sex life a whole new dimension.

Anne, 25

She confesses (boy–girl)

I took my boyfriend to a sex show

One minute Joanne and Matt were lying on the beach, the next they were having hot passionate sex and watching a peep-show.

I blame the sangria. How else would I find myself having the hottest, stickiest sex of my life in a sex-shop booth? OK, I'm adventurous, but that was pushing even *my* limits. It was seedy, sweaty and very, very dirty – and I loved it.

Matt was the type of boyfriend you just die for – stunning, great body, fabulous in bed, fun to be around, and prone to whisking you off for expensive long weekends. Loyal too, and, best of all, no emotional baggage. He was still on speaking terms with his exes, for God's sake. It doesn't get much better than Matt. I'd had a gut-full of guys who switched off, shut down, slept around and/or left a bloody great trail of destruction in their wake. Matt was something else.

We both worked in sales, but we met in a club. Two years on, our sex life was still very hot. This time, he'd taken me to a very exclusive resort on the Spanish coast for a weekend of sunbathing, sangria and, of course, lots of sex.

By Sunday, I was tanned and totally relaxed. Two days spent lying in the sun while Matt rubbed oil all over me every hour had completely chilled me out. Believe me, without that, and far too much sangria, I'd never have ended up in a sex-shop coin-operated booth!

The beach was pretty deserted that Sunday morning. We'd headed down there after a hungover breakfast in our hotel, and by lunchtime we had realised that the only cure was more alcohol. Luckily, the beach-bar waiter strolled around the sun-loungers, taking orders – and tips, as Matt pointed out – so we ordered a huge jug of sangria.

I was sunbathing topless in a thong. We quickly knocked back the sangria and, as if by magic, my thumping headache disappeared. The sun was blazing hot, so Matt rubbed more oil into my back and worked his way down to my thighs. I always got turned on when he did that, but this time he glanced around to see if anyone was looking, especially the waiter, who had lingered a bit too long taking our order. But he was back at the beach bar, and the few other sunbathers were lying down. So Matt slid his fingers inside my thong and stroked them over my clitoris from behind.

The sensation hit me like an electric shock. If our hotel had been nearer, we'd have gone straight back to our room for a session. He masturbated me for almost a minute. I kept my eyes open and it was the horniest, but weirdest, sensation to be so turned on while looking around at the beach and the sea. It felt unreal. I was pretty close to orgasm – and would definitely have come with my eyes open, a first for me – when the waiter decided to walk past. Bloody typical. Maybe he saw what we were up to and wanted a better look. Or maybe he just wanted to top up our sangria while staring at my breasts again. I could have killed him. Matt lay down – awkwardly – on his front and said, 'Quick, talk to me about tax returns.' I was so horny that I had to do something, so I glared at the waiter, put on my top and went to cool off in the sea.

It was a few minutes before Matt could stand up. He waded out to me and gave me a huge kiss. I could see the beach clearly over his shoulder. Everyone was lying down and the waiter had disappeared – nobody was taking any notice of us. The water was just above our waists. Having spent ten minutes waiting for his erection to go down, it suddenly sprang up again in full force. I reached down, slid my thong to one side, and Matt went straight inside me. It was so sudden, and he felt so big inside me, that I couldn't stop myself sliding my hips back and forth. From the beach, with only our top halves visible, I hope we just looked like a couple hugging. Under the water, his penis was sliding in and out over my clitoris, giving me the most incredible sensation. I couldn't believe we were having sex in full view of everyone.

At first he moved gently, but we got faster and faster until we were bobbing up and down in the water. By now I was very horny, but seriously worried that someone would realise what we were up to. So I slid off him, adjusted my thong and went back to the beach, while Matt stayed in the water waiting yet again for his erection to go down.

I'm sure if we'd finished the job, so to speak, I'd never have ended up in a sex shop. But by the time we walked back to the hotel, through the town's alley-ways, I was still horny and on the edge. Easily aroused was an understatement. When we saw the sex shop, Matt and I just had to go in.

It had a tiny entrance, with 'Sex Shop' written in English above it. Matt and I usually go into sex shops for a laugh. Just inside the entrance of this one were several tiny booths. The door to one was open, and I could see a coin-operated TV screen inside. I admit, the idea of sneaking into one of those booths for a quickie turned me on. It was the first place I'd seen all day where we could actually have sex – I wasn't bothered about watching a film. But we went past, giggling, and up the stairs to the main shop.

We had a look through the sex toys. There was no one else in the shop, so I felt we ought to buy something. I chose a set of vibrating balls and a leather bodice, which Matt was especially keen on. On the way back down, I looked at the booths. This was a once-in-a-lifetime chance – I didn't think I'd ever be up for it again. They were pretty small, but I reckoned we'd fit. No one else was around. I couldn't resist whispering, 'Shall we have a quickie?'

The booth was so small that I had to squeeze in and sit on Matt's lap. Air conditioning? No chance. It was boiling inside and we were both horny but, to be honest, at that moment we couldn't stop laughing. Matt locked the door, put a few pesetas in the slot and we watched the show unfold. Actually, 'unfold' isn't the right word – this was full-on from the moment your cash hit the slot.

I'm not into porn, and this was real, continental hardcore stuff. But in that booth, with Matt's erection pressing into me through his thin shorts, the scenes really turned me on. This was hot, dirty, sticky sex, and I loved it. We'd had all kinds of sex in the past, from posh sex in four-posters to quickies in the car.

But this was something else, something new.

I pulled up my skirt, pushed my thong to one side, and Matt slid inside me, masturbating me at the same time. It was the horniest, most satisfying, fun sexual thrill of my life. The film suddenly snapped off and Matt, still inside me, scrabbled around in his pockets searching for more pesetas. When the film came back on, I knew I was going to come quickly. I came hard, and way too loud. Matt took a little longer to come, so I finished our sexual treat by giving him oral sex. He came with a very, very loud grunt.

Afterwards, we were dripping with sweat, claustrophobic, but totally satisfied. The film was still going, and I was still clutching my bag containing the vibrating balls and bodice – I hadn't fancied putting it on the floor. I didn't want anyone to see us leaving the booth, let alone together, so we listened through the door. It was quiet, so Matt slipped out and I followed. Right outside was a middle-aged Spanish man, grinning at us. I didn't look back to see if there were any peep-holes in the door, but we'd definitely given him a very loud sex show. Matt and I were both really embarrassed and practically ran back to the hotel.

I wish I could say Matt and I are still together, but we split up a year later, for all kinds of reasons apart from our sex life. We never forgot our day at the coast. By almost reaching orgasm so many times during the day, when I finally came, it was the best, most explosive, most satisfying climax I've ever had. It still makes me horny when I remember it. I'm sure he gets a kick out of it, too.

Joanne, 25

She confesses (boy–girl)

They caught our sex romp on CCTV

Angie and Paul thought their secret was safe – until friends started calling them 'movie stars' . . .

Paul was 29, gorgeous, and totally out of reach. Engaged, to be precise, but brilliant fun to work with. Brilliant at sex, too, as I found out after one too many vodkas, never dreaming our steamy session was being captured on film for all to see . . .

My acting career had nosedived. Waitressing in a seaside hotel wasn't the most exciting job – lunchtime meant kids screaming for their chicken nuggets, and tea was stuck-up old ladies moaning about their scones. Hardly glamorous, but it paid the bills. Paul made it all worthwhile. He was the head waiter. A struggling actor, too, with Jude Law looks and a wicked sense of humour. He wasn't totally wasted in the hotel. If a customer gave you too much grief, Paul was your man. Even fierce old ladies melted into their cream teas when Paul turned on the charm. Then he'd come into the kitchen, say something truly vile like, 'I bet she hasn't had a good rogering for years,' and sweep back through the swing doors with a beaming smile and complimentary plate of 'chef's best crumpets'. Priceless.

He encouraged me with my acting and let me fit my waitressing around auditions. Things were so bad, I'd even answered an ad in the paper saying 'Actors Wanted'. A fat guy with a cigar offered me the lead role – in a porn film. No thanks. I'm not against porn films, I just didn't want to star in one. Especially if there was any chance of my friends seeing it. Two months later, Paul and I accidentally took the starring role in a porn film watched by most of the waiting staff – and the guys at the nightclub next door.

I'll call it The Empire. It's a huge, sprawling club, packed with anyone who can dress up to look eighteen. The guys are spotty, oversexed and live at home with mum in a bedroom plastered with Pamela Anderson posters. The girls are typical seaside sixteen-year-olds. Too much cheap body spray, blue eyeshadow and knicker lines. The place is to be avoided at all costs. But the new waitress was having her birthday get-together there, so I went. So did Paul.

I didn't think he'd turn up. His girlfriend Nicola was in bed with the flu, so I figured he'd be at home with her. This was the first time I'd ever seen him outside work, and I realised just how much I fancied him. Jen, another waitress, thought it was her lucky night and flirted with him like crazy. I was amazed when he flirted back, so I joined in. Vodka was on special offer and, as the Smirnoff flowed, so did the innuendoes. Paul made it obvious he was interested in me, so Jen went off in a huff. I was too drunk to care – Paul was too good to turn down.

Being mid-week, they'd curtained off the extra seating area at the back of the club. Paul asked if I'd like to go outside, but when we saw the curtains, I couldn't resist poking my head through for a look. All the tables and chairs were empty, so we could have the entire place to ourselves. No one would come back here. I pulled him through the curtains and we kissed. This was raw passion at its best, rough and rude, with loads of swearing. He pulled up my top and teased my nipples with his tongue while I masturbated him through his trousers. Then I unzipped them and gave him oral sex. I'd never had sex with anyone who swore so much, but at the time, it turned on. As I sucked, he described how he was going to have sex with me, how he was going to bend me over the table and take me from behind. I was so horny, I reached down and masturbated.

If I'd been sober, I'd never have done it – not with Paul, and definitely not in a public place. But the drink, the intense sexual attraction, and the fact I'd been single and sex-free for three months, got the better of me. When he was close to climax, he withdrew, pulled me to my feet and bent me over the table. I joined in the swearing, telling him to do it now, fast and hard. I didn't even care that my back was to the curtains. If anyone did look in, I still wouldn't know about it to this day. Paul dug his fingers into my hips and thrust quickly. I brought myself to orgasm with my finger, coming loud and hard. Luckily, the music drowned out Paul's grunts. He felt me orgasm and came with a burst of expletives that were just perfect for that hard, horny sex.

We pulled on our clothes and left the club. Paul offered to walk me home, but I was sobering up and wanted to be on my own. The guilt was kicking in, and so was the hangover. At work the next day, Paul was his usual self, though I had a couple of bitchy comments from Jen. No one seemed to have noticed we'd left the club together. A fight had broken out between two testosterone-laden lads around the time we'd left, so much of the talk was about that. Paul and I didn't need to say anything to each other. We both knew it was a one-night stand, top class, but best not mentioned again.

A week later, Brian, the club's manager, came into the hotel, winked at me and asked when my next movie was coming out. I thought he was being sarcastic about my lack of work, so I gave him a bitchy smile back. Then he disappeared into the office with my supervisor, Jon, who came out and told me to 'hold the fort' while he popped next door. I had no idea what was going on. The club and hotel weren't connected.

Jon spent the afternoon going bright red every time he saw me and going next door with different waiting staff. I thought perhaps the club and hotel were merging, and they were being interviewed for jobs. Why hadn't he asked me? As soon as Paul came on duty, Jon called us both into the office and said if we went next door, Brian had something to show us.

Being daytime, the club had a strange, empty atmosphere.

Brian was sitting in his office, watching what looked like a black-and-white film on a monitor. He grinned and said, 'At least you two weren't anything to do with the fight. I know exactly where you were.' I looked closer at the screen. Paul was facing the camera, and I was on my knees with my back to it giving him a blow-job. The images were all jerky, like something off *Crimewatch*, which made the blow-job look totally bizarre. I blurted out, 'It's not me,' just as I stood up on-screen and faced the camera head-on, before I bent over the table and had the best quickie sex of my life. It was definitely me. Thank God there was no sound on it.

My face was burning red. I didn't know what to do or say. Paul brazened it out. I don't think he realised how many people had seen it. He laughed nervously, said, 'OK, Brian, you've got me. Just don't tell the missus,' and walked back to the hotel. I followed him out and ignored Brian's parting shot of, 'Free admission for you, love. Any time.'

Paul was sweet about it. He asked if I was OK, and said he was really sorry it had happened – not the sex, the tape. That made me feel better. He hoped Nicola wouldn't find out, but if she did, it was his fault for doing it.

I'll never forgive Brian and Jon for showing everyone that tape, and I can't bear to think of the sexual pleasure Brian's got out of it, let alone all his bouncers and anyone else he's shown it to. I'll never have sex in a public place again. Two months on, Paul and I are still the butt of everyone's jokes at least ten times a day. I'll never live it down. They call us 'movie stars'. Nicola hasn't found out so far, but I feel dreadful when she comes to meet Paul from work and the lads talk loudly about 'that movie'. I even heard her ask Paul what film they're always on about. Paul passed it off as 'some porn film they bought mail order'. If only she knew the truth . . .

Angie, 23

Epilogue

So, there you have it – living proof that *Cosmo* readers are girls and boys who just want to have fun. Plane journeys, stage shows, holidays, even a trip to the dentist or a day in the office will never be the same again. Somewhere, right now, a *Cosmo* reader is living out their sexual fantasy – and if they're willing to share it with us, we'll share it with you. If it's hot enough . . .